INDIANS

Edge of a Plains Indian village.
The two boys at the left are training as future
horse thieves by stealing meat
from a drying rack. Their instructor
is their mother's brother. He is beyond
the tepee, mounted.

INDIANS

written and illustrated by EDWIN TUNIS

THE WORLD PUBLISHING COMPANY

CLEVELAND AND NEW YORK

PUBLISHED BY THE WORLD PUBLISHING COMPANY

2231 WEST 110TH STREET, CLEVELAND 2, OHIO

PUBLISHED SIMULTANEOUSLY IN CANADA BY

NELSON, FOSTER & SCOTT LTD.

LIBRARY OF CONGRESS CATALOG CARD NUMBER: 59–7744

for

KRISTIN COX

with

avuncular affection

Platform pipe representing a hawk.
Found in a mound at Hopewell, Ohio.

Acknowledgments

The writer is grateful for the kindness of the personnel of the Enoch Pratt Free Library; the Johns Hopkins University Library; the Peabody Institute Library; the Museum of the American Indian, Haye Foundation; and the Museum of Natural History.

The following individuals have been indispensably helpful: Mr. Eldon W. Amos; Mr. Carl Bryant, Custodian, the Dover Museum; Dr. E. K. Burnett, Director, The Museum of the American Indian, Haye Foundation; Dr. George F. Carter, the Johns Hopkins University; Mr. Harold I. Lessem, the National Park Service; Dr. Herman C. Pitts; Mr. William J. Quinn, Jr.; Dr. F. M. Setzler, Head Curator of Anthropology, the Smithsonian Institution; Dr. Sigmund Spaeth; Mr. William Targ, Vice President of The World Publishing Company.

Special thanks are given to Elizabeth Tunis, my wife, for valuable criticism and for a lot of very hard work.

A short abstract from *Medicine Among the American Indians*, by Dr. Eric Stone, is made by permission of the publishers, Paul B. Hoeber, Inc.

E. T.

Long Last
July 25, 1958

Contents

Illustrations

Foreword

Your author is no anthropologist, but he can read and he has done so. The subject of the American Indian is endlessly fascinating, and a vast number of books have been written about it. Some of them are minute accounts of minor tribes, and others are frustratingly vague because they can't help being so. The most vague accounts are those about the eastern Indians, long since uprooted by the European invasion. The new Americans didn't begin to study the old ones much before 1880, and by then a lot had been lost forever.

The Indians themselves have forgotten most of their past. None of them now chip flint arrowheads, and few of them have any idea that their forefathers did so. Some old ways do survive, but it seemed best to write this account in the past tense to avoid having to note exceptions continually.

Our concern in this book is with the day-to-day living of the Indians and their ways of doing things before they met the white man—with one exception: The culture of the Plains Indians resulted from the white man's horses; but those were not obtained directly, and in every other way the whole thing was Indian. Since everything about the Indians can't go into one volume, this one has nothing to say about their sorry history after white settlement began, little about their mythology and legends, and little more about ceremonials; but we are still left with something to talk about.

Indian tribes were numbered by hundreds; so we shall consider kinds of Indians rather than tribes. It has usually happened, however, that the text for any particular culture is based on one or two tribes that best represent their area or about whom information is available. Unquestionably errors of detail occur, as they seem to do even in some scholarly works on the subject. The author regrets such errors, especially those that may result from his ignorance.

The illustrations try to re-create bits of daily life, unromanticized, and as few liberties as possible have been taken with known facts. Sometimes it has been necessary to resort to reasonable probability, however, and these instances are noted in the captions whenever this has been done to any major extent. Some examples of Indian art appear incidentally in the illustrations, but there is no attempt to render it in detail for the reason that, copied by another hand, it is no longer Indian art.

It seems that we should not look upon the Indians as savages but as fellow men, a little, but only a little, slower in developing than we. After all, they were living in ways not too different from those described in the following pages when some of our ancestors, robed in skins and with their bodies painted a tasteful blue, were appeasing the gods with bloody sacrifices of fellow clansmen at Stonehenge. We have had the better opportunities since then; but we are not necessarily very different people.

The Indians lived over almost all of this continent. Many museums have fine collections of their crafts. If after reading this book you look at them a little more closely and with a little more understanding, *Indians* will have achieved its modest purpose.

Cochise pod corn (actual size)

1

Earliest Americans

No race of men originated in America. Neither the bones of primordial man nor of the great apes that preceded him have been found here. But man has been here a long time. Charcoal from one of his campfires has been shown from its radioactivity to be at least 35,000 years old, and Dr. George F. Carter has found other traces that suggest man's presence perhaps even before the last glacier covered the northern half of the continent.

Authorities no longer argue as to how men came into America. They crossed dryshod from Asia on an isthmus exposed across what is now Bering Strait when glacial ice had captured much of the world's water and lowered the level of the sea. The chances are that many of the immigrants didn't realize they had crossed anything. Hunting, they followed the musk ox; fleeing from pursuit, they escaped into a new world which was to them only more of the old one. Their dogs were the only

domestic animals that came with them. There was never any mass migration apparently, only a continuing and fluctuating drift.

Since these people came out of Asia, it was formerly assumed that they were Mongoloids, related to the present Mongolians; hence, all American Indians must of necessity be Mongoloids. It now appears that the very early Asiatics were not themselves all Mongoloids; other races lived in that region or at least passed through it.

Some 10,000 years ago nomad hunters, called by us the Folsom people, left their unmistakable spear points spread in a broad band across the middle of the United States, almost from coast to coast. They hunted the mammoth and drove herds of giant bison over cliffs.

Folsom men made some of the best spearheads that have ever been found anywhere; but there are no traces of their dwellings, and no pottery

Roughing out with a hammerstone

Finishing with a bone flaking tool

has been identified as theirs. Recently a presumed Folsom skull was discovered.

Flint-knapping

Some glassy stones, like flint and obsidian, which contain no impurities can be shaped rather handily; any flake chipped from them, large or small, will always be the same shape, something like that of one side of a clam shell. The American Indians knew this and made use of it. Crude spearheads and arrowheads were shaped by knocking the flakes off with a hammerstone, for which almost any old rock that fit the hand would serve.

A rough point could be touched up and refined by removing smaller flakes from around its edges. Not all Indians knew how to do this; or else they knew, but didn't bother. The small flakes could be chipped off by simple pressure from a tool held in the hand. The tool was a bluntish point of horn or bone. Holding the roughed-out flint against a chunk of wood or even against the protected heel of his left hand, the arrowsmith pressed his horn point downward on the edge of the flint's upper surface and popped a small flake from its *underside*. Folsom man was a complete master of this craft, so deft in fact that no one has satisfactorily explained how he was able to flake out, at one blow for each, the neat troughs he made on both faces of his javelin heads; but he did it.

Prehistoric Farmers

The second group of very ancient Americans have been named the Cochise. They settled in the Southwest and stayed home to gather nuts and hunt small local game. In the latter part of their long "history," about 5,000 years ago, they raised tobacco and a primitive kind of corn, each kernel of which was covered with its own separate husk.

These people chipped flint spearheads that are strikingly like those of the prehistoric cave painters in Europe. They used the atlatl, or spear thrower, which was also used by the cave painters, by the Aztecs (*atlatl* is an Aztec word), by the Australian aborigines, and which some American Indians abandoned only when they could get guns. Folsom men probably had spear throwers, too.

The Spear Thrower

An atlatl was a shaped stick about two feet long, an inch or so wide, and about half that thick. One end was formed into a handle and was sometimes wrapped with cord. At the top of the handle two notches, or sometimes two loops, provided finger grips. At the upper end of the stick a recess made a purchase for the butt of the spear; sometimes the same objective was served by a spur, usually an animal tooth set in the wood.

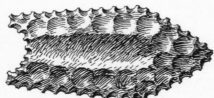

Folsom javelin point

16

A stone weight was attached to the atlatl near its upper end as a help in throwing. Stones for this purpose were carefully shaped so that one side wouldn't be heavier than the other. Such stones, of many patterns, are found at Indian archaeological sites and for years nobody could figure out what they were; they were labeled "banner stones," "butterfly stones," or "problematical objects." The mystery was solved when atlatls, with their banner stones still in place, were found in caves in Kentucky and Alabama.

The atlatl spear, or javelin, was quite long, from six to nine feet. It was headed with either a sharp flint point or a rounded "bunt" of bone or wood, that was better for killing birds and small animals because it didn't tear the flesh. Either kind was usually attached to a short foreshaft that fitted into a socket in the main shaft. Streamers were often tied to the butt of such a spear to help its flight, to aid in recovery, or just for excitement.

In throwing, the javelin was supported by the left hand while the right, holding the atlatl, reached back until throwing stick and spear were parallel. The spear lay above the stick and between the first and second fingers of the hunter's right hand where they held the throwing grips. Launching was done with a straight overhand swing, the left hand letting go of the spear as soon as there was thrust behind it.

The Influx Continues

About 4,500 years ago the Algonquian people began to come into America, and they kept up their immigration for 2,000 years, spreading eastward above and below the Great Lakes. Their pottery, patterned with a cord-wrapped paddle, and their polished stone axes can be traced from the Atlantic to the Atlantic again, across Europe, Asia, and North America. Some believe that they stem from the dark branch of the white race which originated in Spain. They brought bows and arrows with them but not necessarily the earliest ones.

After the Algonquians and perhaps partly with them, the Mongoloids came in successive waves, filling up the empty spaces. Some went on down into Mexico; some went into the Mississippi Valley; others settled between the Rocky Mountains and the Pacific Coast Range; others, the Athapascans, stopped in Canada; and still other Mongoloids—the Eskimos—were left in the Arctic.

All of these different people, mixed up a little by interbreeding, are called Indians. To consider them a single race, as we thoughtlessly have done, is absurd. They differ among themselves in language, in appearance, and in customs far more radically than do the nations of Europe. Even the color of their skins varies widely.

For many years ethnologists believed that the Indians invented their ways of doing things quite independently of other people in the world who, faced with the same problems, solved them in identical ways. The newer diffusion theory holds that the human race isn't really very inventive; once an idea is hit upon, it spreads from one group to another. It is thought to be highly unlikely that an idea will be duplicated independently by a people who are cut off from the normal chain of contact. In the light of this, it is believed that our Indians either brought their basic ideas with them, learned ideas from other Indians who had imported them originally, or had contact *long after migration to America* with Asia, Polynesia, and possibly with Europe. This last theory is no pipe dream; it has the support of some serious and respected scientists.

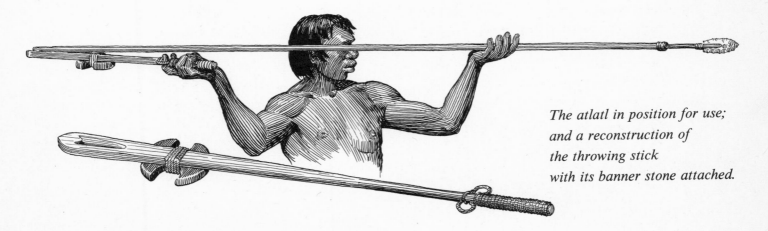

The atlatl in position for use; and a reconstruction of the throwing stick with its banner stone attached.

The Basketmakers

The climate of the Southwest was dry enough, even when the Cochise lived there, to preserve any article that was left in a cave. Even wooden objects and woven fabrics have been found in nearly unchanged condition. It is because of this that quite a lot is known about the Cochise and about their successors in the area, whom we call the Basketmakers because beautiful examples of their baskets survive.

The Basketmakers took up about where the Cochise left off, sometime about the year A.D. I. Their villages were located near the opening of a cave. The cave was used for storage and as a place to work, out of the heat of the sun. Living was mostly out of doors, but there were casual huts of brush where the people slept.

Pits dug in the floors of the caves were used as rainproof bins for corn. They were so successful that ears of perfectly preserved Basketmaker corn have been found in them. Though its ears are small, seldom much more than four inches long, careful breeding had vastly improved the Basketmaker corn over the pod corn of the Cochise. Its grains were now covered by a husk that enclosed the whole ear.

In time, the Basketmakers improved their houses by adapting the form of the storage pits. They lined a pit with stones and gave it a flat roof with slanting sides covered with brush and mud. A central hole served as both door and smoke outlet.

A second group of people peaceably joined the original Basketmakers about A.D. 500 and started

A Basketmaker pit house

making changes. The caves and the pit houses were abandoned, and mud houses were built in the open. These came to be joined together to form a semicircle. They were the first pueblos. In the court there were always one or two of the old pit structures that may have been used for storage or may, even then, have served as meeting and loafing places for the men, as did the sacred and woman-free kivas of the later pueblos.

The Old Towns

In time, stone as well as mud began to be used for building, and the pueblos grew in size. Pueblo Bonito in what is now New Mexico was built about A.D. 920. Its stonework was superb. It had more than 500 rooms arranged in tiers, like a great stair, leading upward from the arc of a semicircular court. The sheer wall at the back was five stories high. But Pueblo Bonito stood in a plain and was open to attack from all sides. Its farming inhabitants gave up after two centuries and built themselves stone houses in cliff recesses high on the sides of mesas.

Crops were grown in safety on the flat tops of the mesas, but they had only such moisture as prayer and ceremony could wring from the gods. It was a 23-year drought that drove the cliff dwellers into the valleys again late in the thirteenth century.

The Mound Builders

Hundreds of large mounds still exist in the east-central United States, particularly in the valleys of the Ohio and Mississippi rivers. They were once thought to be relics of a great civilization perhaps more advanced than that of the Aztecs. Careful study has now shown the builders of them to have been merely farming Indians who were exceptionally good craftsmen in some fields and who held strong ideas on social rank. The more northern mounds were tombs, apparently reserved for aristocrats. These Indians dredged fresh-water

A Mound Builder aristocrat arrayed in beaten copper and freshwater pearls

pearls from the rivers. Important people wore quantities of the pearls as ornaments and they may also have served as trade articles, because copper, mica, shark teeth, and conch shells found in the mounds obviously came from distant sources.

The burial-mound people flourished over 3,000 years ago, and what it was that disrupted them is a mystery. It could have been invasion or an epidemic; or the exhaustion of their farm lands (this reason has been guessed for the desertion of Mayan cities); or it could have been a slave revolt, for they almost certainly held slaves.

Compared to their craftsmanship in metal and stone, the pottery of the burial-mound people was crude; but to the south of them there were other mound builders who were superb potters. These southern mounds were seldom graves. They were the bases for wooden temples and were primitive reproductions of the pyramids of Mexico. The temple-mound art style, too, shows strong evidence of some remote connection with the Mexican Indians. Remnants of the temple-mound culture survived into historical times among the Muskhogean Indians of the Southeast and there are broad hints of a connection between the burial-mound people and the Iroquoians.

2

The Indians as People

It's dangerous to generalize about Indians. Someone who knows what he's talking about may rise up and contradict you flatly; there seems always to be an exception or so to any general statement about them. Nevertheless, some things are *nearly* true of most Indians. This section is for those things.

North America has widely differing areas of climate, of soil, and of terrain. The Indians occupying the various sections had perforce to work out ways of surviving in them. They became specialized Indians: woods hunters, plains hunters, fishermen, farmers, and wild-seed eaters. This is an arbitrary way of stating the case. Most of the hunters raised some corn, and the others did some hunting.

It's believed that there were about a million Indians on the North American continent when the first Europeans arrived. They were widely scattered; some sections of the country were nearly empty. Unfortunately for the twentieth-century student, the Indians were far from consistent in grouping themselves. It would seem reasonable for the people in any one section of the country to speak a similar language, but that would be too easy; the Indians mixed things up.

Languages and Communication

The majority of the Indians who spoke dialects of the language family called Athapascan hunted caribou. But there were Athapascan tribes who were not caribou hunters and whose way of life was totally different; some lived in Arizona and New Mexico, some on the California coast. There were Sioux-speaking Indians in Virginia who knew little about hunting buffalo; and there were Algonquians, speaking forms of the language of the New England woodsmen, who *did* hunt buffalo on the western plains. In upper New York State was the great "island" of Iroquois tribes, speaking a tongue that had its roots far away and which was unintelligible to the Algonquians who surrounded the Iroquois. These are only a few examples. All of these transplanted Indians clung to their own language, even though they tended to adopt the

20

ways of their neighbors because those ways suited the nature of the country.

A detached tribe modified its words to suit itself, but kept the grammatical structure of the parent language intact. It is this latter fact that has enabled scholars to assign memberships in the basic language families. An example of the changes that distance—even a few miles—could make in language may be found in the Five Nations of the Iroquois. Each of the five was in constant touch with the others; they were all of one blood and, alone of any considerable tribal group, they had a common government. Each of the nations could make shift to understand the others, yet their words for the same things were pronounced quite differently, so much so that the differences show up clearly in the attempts made to spell the words with English letters.

When man first spoke he used single words, perhaps grunts accompanied by gestures to complete his meaning. When the need arose to express two or more associated ideas, the problem was solved by joining together the words for the separate ideas into a single new word, with perhaps a nonessential syllable or so left out. Sometimes the original meanings were stretched pretty far. Using this system, Indians had no trouble coining apt words for things they'd never seen before; for example, they produced a word for steamboat that meant "walks-on-the-water."

In his book *The American Race,* Dr. Daniel G. Brinton gives an example of the growth of words by combination. It was taken from the Lenape, an Algonquian language, and part of it goes something like this:

Starting with

NI: *I, my, mine, we, our* and adding HILLAN: *it is true,* gave

NÍ HILLAN: *mine, it is true; this is truly mine.* This was also a verb,

NÍ HILLAN: *I beat,* because what is mine I may beat. With the accent shifted, the meaning was intensified; it became

NIHIĹ LAN: *beat to death, kill.* But a different addition could change the whole meaning. Adding APE (aṕ-ë): *a man* (and dropping part of the old word) gave

NIHIL LAṔE: *I, it is true, a man;* that is, *my own master.*

The names we have for most Indian tribes are those by which other tribes called them or those

21

Western Blackfoot and
Eastern Lenape, Algonquians both

given them by Europeans. Their names for themselves almost always meant "the men" or "the people." It took their neighbors to hit upon descriptive names, often not very complimentary. About thirty different Indian names are listed for the Dakota Indians, and a fair percentage of them can be translated to mean "cutthroats." Quite often the name conferred on a neighboring tribe meant, "they talk gibberish."

The Indians of the western Plains developed a formal gesture language by which tribes of differing speech could communicate. Though it wasn't known far outside that area, probably any Indian could have understood it pretty well, since much of it was pantomime and any Indian was a good actor.

The Maya of Mexico were the only Indians who achieved a written language, with symbols that stood for individual words, but some of the North American Indians showed signs of heading in that

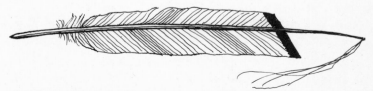

Dakota honor feather
meaning the wearer had cut an enemy's throat

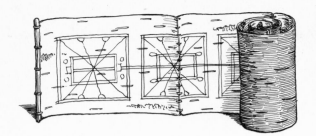

Birch-bark roll recording ceremonies
of the Chippewa Midewiwin society

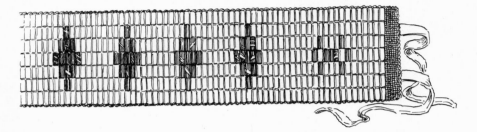

Part of an Iroquois wampum belt

direction when the first white men arrived. The Chippewa scratched marks on strips of birch bark to record the ceremonies of their secret society, the Midewiwin. These could be interpreted readily by an initiate. The Lenape (Delawares) painted red marks upon sticks. The Iroquois recorded events with wampum. In all three cases the pattern jogged the memory; the story or the treaty was learned by rote and repeated verbatim.

Most Indians did picture-writing on stones and other surfaces, but most of the marks are beyond our interpretation. Quite a few of these were never anything but doodles or bids for luck. The exploit pictures that the Dakota men painted on their tepees are understood, and so are their "winter counts." There are hints of meaning in some scratchings done in the East, but none that tells us anything much of Indian history. Quite a few of them may have been made secretly by medicine men who then claimed supernatural origin for them.

There was another very practical kind of picture-writing in use among the woodland Indians. By it a hunter could leave a message at his camp to show which way he had gone, what he was going to do, and how long he would be away; but the reader had to guess when he had left. There was no way to indicate the date except by scratching an indication of the phase of the moon, though no example of this is known.

Physical Characteristics

The fact that all Indians didn't have a common origin is borne out by the differences in their physical appearance. There were tribes who tended to be tall and spare; those who were short and stocky; and those, like the Ute, who tended to be fat. Some Indians had broad faces and noses and thick lips; others had narrow faces, eaglelike noses, and very thin lips. These were tribal characteristics, not those of individuals. Skin colors differed, too. First of all, no Indian, except a freshly sunburned one or a painted one, was red; mostly they were tan. Some were dark to the point of being definitely brown; others were as light as an Italian or a Spaniard. The parts of the body that were exposed to the sun (usually most

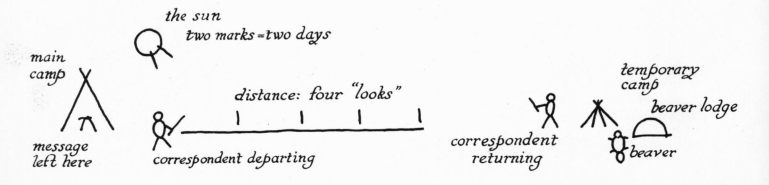

Diagram of a Penobscot birch-bark "letter"
Translation: "Gone to my beaver-trapping camp, four looks away. Back in two days."

A variety of physical types; they are all called Indians

Mahican

Northeastern forest hunter

Hopi

Southwestern desert farmer

Haida

Northwestern coast fisherman

Navaho

Southwestern desert hunter

Dakota

Western Plains hunter

of it) were darker, as is the white man's under these conditions. The Indians themselves have remarked that most Europeans are redder than they are.

Nearly all Indians had coarse black hair. Usually the hair was perfectly straight, but sometimes it was wavy. Two things were rare: a bald Indian and a left-handed one.

It's not quite true that all Indians were beardless. Most of them had scant facial hair, which they pulled out; but occasionally there was an Indian with a small beard. On the Northwest coast the men habitually wore beards and mustaches. Theirs grew thicker than the beards of most Indians.

Tattooed chin

Skin Decoration

The fact that Indians painted their faces and bodies is well-known. In war they did it with the idea of making themselves look ferocious, an object it served very well. Painting was also used as ornament, designs for ceremonials being applied according to fancy. Body paint was sometimes patterned by dragging the finger tips through it. An over-all coat of paint was often worn for no other purpose than to protect the skin from the

A Southeastern Indian painted for battle

sun. Women did this even more frequently than men. The powdered paint was usually mixed with grease and applied as a salve, but often it was applied to the skin dry over a coat of grease that was likely to be fish oil or eagle fat. Some vegetable juices were used as body paint, but most of it came from colored clays, red ocher being the most common. Black was powdered charcoal.

Some Indians, but only some of them, went in for tattooing. When they did, the designs were usually made by rubbing soot into deep scratches. The marks left are said to have looked bluish on the skin. A favorite subject for tattooing was the animal that served as the distinguishing mark of the clan, the totem, or one that served the individual as his private protector. There was much tattooing in the South and the far West. In parts of the Northwest it was done over most of the body and was beautifully executed. Here, a few vertical lines on a woman's chin were felt to be necessary for real beauty.

Health

The Indians were not completely healthy, though they missed a good many of the white man's miseries, at least until he brought them in. They had no resistance to contagious diseases such as smallpox; and even measles could decimate an Indian tribe. So susceptible were they to infection that they could catch smallpox from a healthy white man who merely camped near them and with whom they had no direct contact whatever.

Cancer in an Indian is still rare, and there is no recorded case from early days. Most of their

24

physical troubles were the result of the lives they led. Gorging after starvation gave them indigestion. Dampness and cold gave them rheumatism and neuralgia, pleurisy and pneumonia. Smoky lodges gave them sore eyes.

Much of the Indian's treatment for sickness was magical hocus-pocus. But much of it was also intelligent and effective, even though it was likely to be applied to symptoms rather than to causes. Magic was called upon when knowledge failed. There is a tradition of a vast Indian herb lore. Much of this is romantic nonsense, but not all of it; in *Medicine Among the American Indians*, Dr. Eric Stone says that modern doctors have made use of fifty-nine Indian herbs. Dr. Stone's book is the source of many of the facts in this section.

The Indians were exceptionally good at treating wounds and could effectively suture large ones. They also set broken bones and splinted them, and they relieved dislocations. There is a known case of an Indian who, by tying his foot to a tree, was able to get his own hip joint back into place. The average Indian's knowledge of human anatomy was far greater than that of most of the white settlers.

Men, women, and children lived strenuous lives that lasted about as long as ours, and probably longer than those of Europeans at that time. They could accomplish remarkable feats of endurance. Any young Indian runner could cover a hundred miles in a day, and there are attested cases of their doing considerably more. The Penobscots kept certain of their young men in strict training for running down deer! This was a matter of staying power, not speed. Even today an elderly Hopi will jog trot twenty miles to his cornfield, work all day, and jog home again.

Indians are credited with phenomenal eyesight. There's no evidence that their eyes were physically different or better than other human eyes; they simply knew how, and for what, to look. A white man who has spent his life at sea will spot a buoy far sooner than a landlubber; and one who has lived in the woods can see a squirrel's eye where a city man sees only leaves.

The Nature of the Indian

A standard libel on the Indians was expressed in a popular song of the early 1900's, "Let the women do the work . . . while the men sit around all day." Indian women did work hard, but so did the men. The women kept house—in fact, they often *owned* the house—and keeping it included carrying water, cutting firewood, tanning

Penobscot "pure man" running down a deer

The social amenities

leather, and a lot of other things that aren't now considered a part of housekeeping. If there was any farming done, they usually did it. Possibly it was the women who originally began farming in an attempt to steady the food supply. The job of the men was providing meat, and since game was scattered, finding it and stalking it took time and intense effort. When a man was at home he loafed and rested except when he was making or repairing hunting equipment, which took considerable doing. Nor did he wait to go hunting until the spirit moved him; twenty-five people could eat a deer in a day.

The sentimental picture of the Indian as "the noble red man" and the prejudiced one of him as "the vicious savage" were both equally distorted. He was simply a human being, living his own special kind of life, and his acts were consistent with his knowledge, his traditions, and his environment. Individually, the Indians showed the same variations of character, good and bad, that are found in other races. Collectively, they were generous and limitlessly hospitable. They looked with disgusted contempt upon the white man who wouldn't share his house, his food, and his pipe with friend or stranger, as any Indian would. Even a declared enemy who came in peace to an Indian lodge was fed and given a place to sleep in complete security.

Manners

Few Europeans who dealt with Indians ever got beyond the "poker face" that an Indian presented in public. Even the children could suppress laughter completely and would show no trace of curiosity in the presence of a stranger. An Indian husband returning from a long absence would greet his family, whom he loved and with whom he was privately kind and playful, showing all the animation of the Sphinx; and they, overjoyed, would give back the same impassive stare.

When a stranger or a friend entered an Indian lodge he met the same frozen countenances. A short word of greeting from the host—"You have come?" "Yes, I have come."—a gesture to a seat, and a massive period of silence; this was Indian politeness. It embarrassed white men, to whom silence is intolerable. Presently a pipe would be lighted and passed to the guest, and after a short time, conversation would begin. If the visitor was well-known to the household, everybody would relax, chattering and laughing, for the Indian was not taciturn among his friends. Years ago a delegation of Dakotas was taken to a vaudeville theater in Washington, D.C. They loved it. Under the spell of the darkened auditorium their dignified reserve melted, and their joyous whoops nearly broke up the show.

26

Religion and Superstition

Much, possibly too much, has been written about Indian religion and mythology. It is proposed to add very little to that mass of material here. From the first, Europeans tried to see in the Indian beliefs parallels to their own, and inevitably they imagined likenesses that didn't really exist; just as some of them were able to cook up all sorts of "proofs" that the Indians were descended from one of the lost tribes of Israel, or that some of them were Welsh!

The major religious belief grafted upon these people by the white men was "the Great Spirit," a God above gods. This idea sounded all right to the Indian, and he accepted it with no trouble at all. He believed in everything, and he was quite used to tribal beliefs that differed in detail from his own. Soon, he came to think that the Great Spirit had always been a part of Indian religion.

Actually, aboriginal religious ideas varied with the needs of the peoples' lives. All of the Indians' gods were personifications of nature, but they did not conceive of the universe itself as God in the sense that is called pantheism. In most cases the chief god was the sun, because all that was beneficial seemed to come ultimately from that source. There were gods for each of the winds; in fact, the Four Directions (and sometimes six, including up and down) were constant factors in ceremonies and in the decorations that were applied to baskets, pots, and many other tools and utensils. In the arid sections of the country, the rain gods were the principal deities; there the sun didn't have to be encouraged to shine. There were also evil gods of whirlwind and lightning who must be propitiated for the saving of Indian skins.

The Indians deified animals, particularly game animals, in the belief that there was a super deer, a super buffalo, well disposed toward men, which

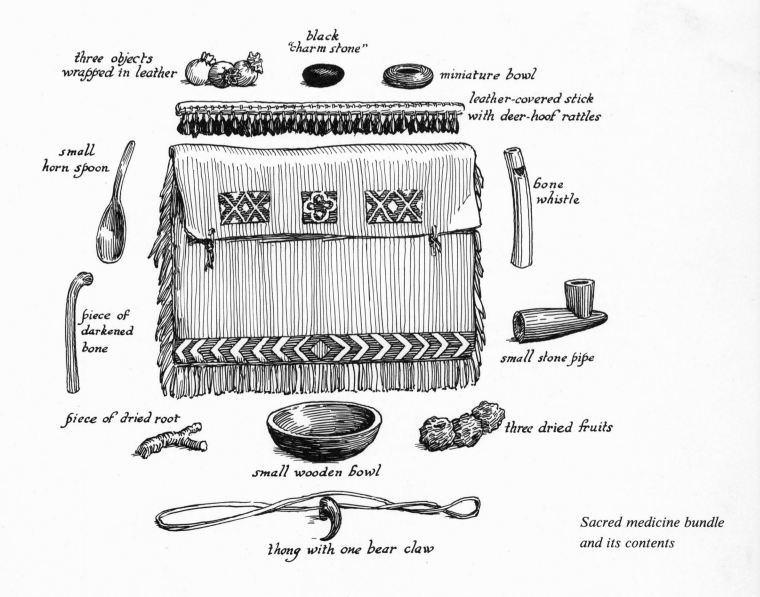

three objects wrapped in leather

black "charm stone"

miniature bowl

leather-covered stick with deer-hoof rattles

small horn spoon

bone whistle

piece of darkened bone

small stone pipe

piece of dried root

three dried fruits

small wooden bowl

thong with one bear claw

Sacred medicine bundle and its contents

Grave of an early Chippewa.
Five lines on the cedar
marker count the scalps he
took. His clan totem, a
marten, is head-downward in
sign of death.
Nothing whatever gives a
hint of his name.

when rightly cajoled would see that hunting was successful. Animals were deified in another sense, too. Each clan within the tribe had its own totem animal, which was usually thought of as the supernatural ancestor of the family and as its protector. Each man also had a personal animal guardian whose species he would not kill. This was the manitou, acquired in youth from a dream which was deliberately courted after fasting and purification.

Most Indians believed in survival after death, and perhaps the traditional phrase "happy hunting grounds" expresses their idea of it pretty well. Afterlife was a replica of life on earth, with the hardships left out. It was all rather vague: the ghosts of men hunting the ghosts of animals. Some Indians believed that spirits grew old in the land of the dead and were then reborn on earth.

Indian attitudes toward the dead, both the corpse and the spirit, differed widely across the country. Cremation was known in which a man's house and all of his belongings were burned up with him. In many tribes bodies were placed on scaffolds, out of reach of animals. As a rule the nomadic tribes simply left the bodies there; the more settled tribes recovered the bones later and

buried them or preserved them in grisly piety. By and large, the agriculturists and the woods hunters lived happily with their dead, ascribing to them a beneficent interest in human welfare. Many of the Plains hunters and all of the Digger Indians of the West were ghost-ridden and terrified of the dead.

There was no Indian who was even reasonably free from superstition; it covered everything in the world. When every animal and every tree, every stream and every natural phenomenon was possessed of a spirit, probably malevolent, it took a lot of finger-crossing and wood-knocking to ward off evil. The Indian was afraid of everything. He was afraid of killing snakes and wolves. He was afraid of witchcraft and of the owls he associated with it. Other examples of superstition will crop up in this book, because it pervaded all Indian living.

Human sacrifice for religious reasons wasn't unknown, but it occurred only in a very few tribes. Cannibalism, too, is reported in at least two parts of the country: in the Great Basin region of the West, where it was brought about by starvation, as it was with some white people later; and along the Texas coast, where a few small tribes had a well-developed taste for "long pig."

The Indian and the White Man

Drinking was no problem among the Indians before the white men came. There were some dreadful native concoctions made, but few of them were alcoholic. It was the early fur traders who, in their avarice, gave the Indians guns and liquor. Indians simply could not handle rum, nor could they resist it. They were maddened by it. They "threw each other in the fire." When they got hold of any, they drank until it was all gone or until they passed out. The wiser old men pleaded with the whites to withhold the stuff, and some of their pleas are touching.

The presence of the English colonists didn't worry the Indians at first. What were a few more people to share the hunting grounds? Later, they naturally felt fierce resentment at the destruction of those hunting grounds. The Eastern Indians were pushed westward, and their pressure disrupted tribes that had never seen a white man. Along the frontier a bitter war raged sporadically for the better part of two centuries. Abominable things were done by both sides, as can be read in some—but not all— history books. It would seem that, of the two opponents, the Indian had the better excuses: He was fighting a desperate fight; his country was being taken away from him; and nothing in his education had taught him forbearance or kindness to his enemies.

The white man, in spite of his golden rule, was the aggressor and the thief. His cruelties are not to be condoned; and yet——Suppose we—you and I—had just found this continent today, rich and untouched. What would we do about it? Sail away and leave the Indians in peace? We would not! We'd take it away from them.

Felling a tree

3

The Woodland Hunters

Before 1607 the eastern half of North America was largely covered with what ecologists call climax forest. In each section of this region the kinds of trees best suited to its climate and soil had won out over all others and stood, decently spaced and of maximum size, in a grandeur that we can only imagine.

The Indians commonly let the trees stand where they grew, because they were so big that felling one was a major undertaking. When a large log was needed—perhaps for a dugout canoe—the only way to get it was by the risky method of burning the tree down. Stone axes weren't equal to the job, though they helped. Before burning down a tree, a band of wet clay was plastered around it a couple of feet from the ground as a firestop. Then the space below the clay was ringed with fire, which was fueled and fanned until it had eaten through the bole. Chipping out charred wood

hastened things a little; that's where the stone ax came in.

Stone axes weren't made of the glassy kinds of rock that flake uniformly; the more granular rocks that are actually mixtures of several minerals were used for them. These stones were shaped by pecking off little bits, using another stone as a hammer; then grinding the surface smooth with sandstone and, finally, polishing it. Decomposed limestone or charcoal made good polishers. The time needed to complete an ax head varied with the hardness of the stone; it's been done in four and a half hours, polishing included.

Some stone ax heads were grooved deeply all the way around the middle; others were grooved on the sides and top but not on the bottom; still others had no groove whatever. A tribe ordinarily made all of its axes the same way. The form of the groove, or its absence, depended on how the

30

handle was to be attached. The head could be lashed to the flat end of a stick (three-quarter groove); it could be lashed into a cleft stick (full groove); it could be wedged into a hole made through one end of a stick (no groove); it could even be *grown* into its handle by leaving it for a year or two in a split made through a growing branch. In time, the split would heal around it and hold it very tight.

The handle of the ax was never put through a hole in the stone head, because a hole weakened the head too much; not because a hole couldn't be drilled in stone; that could be, and was, done. A hollow reed, turned by a bowstring and fed constantly with sand and water, would do the trick. The reed wore out pretty fast, but there were plenty of reeds. Stone was sawed in a similar way, by feeding sand and water to a rawhide bowstring.

A stone ax wasn't only a tool; it was also a weapon. It was the original tomahawk. It could be used as a battle-ax, or thrown as a missile. The tomahawk we ordinarily associate with Indians was a metal trade article manufactured in England, France, or Spain. Each of these nations had its own designs, usually including a pipe bowl that could be smoked through the haft!

In addition to axes and unhafted stone hammers the woodland Indians made chisels and gouges of stone for woodworking, but they were clumsy things compared to the "crooked knife" that every man owned. Its handle was curved to suit the special way it was held and the blade, a beaver's tooth, was curved also, because that's the way beaver teeth grow. The handle was gripped,

Pecking

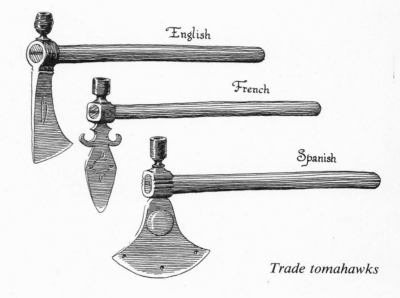

English

French

Spanish

Trade tomahawks

Stone axes

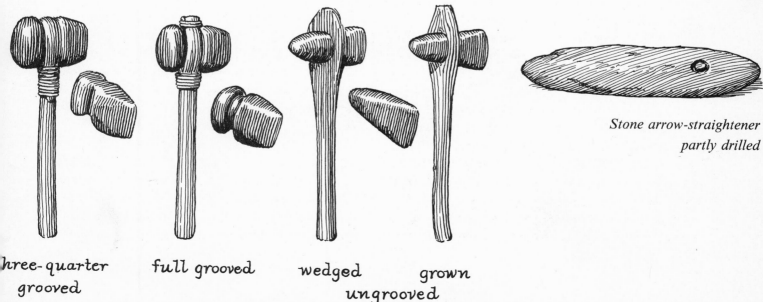

hree-quarter grooved

full grooved

wedged ungrooved

grown

Stone arrow-straightener partly drilled

palm down, with the thumb resting against the turned-over end and the blade projecting on the little-finger side. Cutting was done by pulling the blade toward the user's body. Beavers cut down trees with their teeth. While the best part of the long tooth is its natural cutting edge at the bottom, the whole thing is hard enough to stand grinding to real keenness.

All of the Eastern Indians lived in the woods and all of them hunted, but those of the southern woodlands depended on farming for food far more than on game; and they were very different people. The northern hunters are the concern of this section. Roughly, their area extended from the latitude of the bottom of Hudson's Bay to that of Cape Hatteras. Most of the hunters spoke Algonquian dialects and were of that racial strain. The term Algonquian comes from Algonquin, the name of one band of one tribe. The exception to the Algonquian rule in the woods was the Iroquois. They deserve a place to themselves and shall get it.

People who depend on game for a living can't dwell in large towns; the animals are too scattered. So the hunting tribes were spread out. The members of each tribe acknowledged common bonds and assembled once or twice a year for a powwow (an Algonquian word and idea). Beyond that there was little tribal organization, though there was a tendency to subdivide into bands. The bands divided into villages of a hundred or less. The reason there were so many Indian chiefs is that the leader of each village was given the title.

The woodland area covered a lot of space, and conditions within it varied enough to make differences between tribes in their ways of life. The northern tribes could build birch-bark canoes and embroider their clothes with moose hair; south of New York State the Algonquians had to content themselves with dugout canoes. They never saw

a moose, though they could sometimes bag a buffalo not too far from the Atlantic coast. Some tribes could catch fish in quantity, and it was an important part of their food; others had so few fish near them that they didn't consider it fit to eat.

Shelter

The Mahicans and a few other Algonquians adopted the kind of bark apartment building that the Iroquois called a longhouse, but most tribes did too much seasonal moving to make a communal dwelling practical. A single family occupied an Algonquian wigwam. There were three styles: domed, conical, and what might be called extended conical. There seems to have been a quonset-shaped house, too, in Virginia and North Carolina. All of them were made with a framework of poles and covered with bark or mats, or both.

The domed house, the true *wigiwam* of the Chippewas, was the most common type. Its plan was circular or slightly oval. The diameter of a round one was usually about fifteen feet. To frame a domed lodge, some sixteen or twenty long poles were set firmly in the ground on its perimeter. They were so arranged that each pole had its mate directly opposite it, across the circle. Most of the poles were set about two feet apart, but at four equidistant points on the circumference, pairs of them were set only one foot apart. The tops of the poles were sprung inward, and mates were lashed together to form a rectangular grid of arches. The lashing was done with strips of linden or cedar bark. Wherever two of the arches crossed, they were firmly tied together.

Just at the tops of the four low arches made by the close-set poles, and about six feet from the ground, a horizontal ring of overlapping saplings was lashed around the house, completely encircling it. Below this, two or three other rings were put on. These didn't quite complete the circuit; they skipped a space between two arches to make a doorway. Cutting poles and building the frame was man's work.

The kind of sheathing used on the wigwam varied a little according to locality. Frequently, the walls were covered with mats made of cattail rushes, sewn together by the women. The roof was bark. Chestnut, oak, and elm would serve, but

32

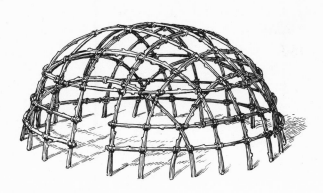

Frame for a domed wigwam

Domed wigwam

birch was the best; it was light and hence handy to roll up and take along when the family moved. Often, a wigwam was covered with several different materials. In cold weather the Chippewas used a layer of bark over a layer of mats, and then banked leaves against the lodge and piled evergreen branches over them.

When birch bark was used, three-foot sections of it were sewn together side by side to make mats ten or twelve feet long. Sticks were fastened across both ends of the mats to keep the bark from splitting. Birch bark tends to split around the tree, instead of up and down, so the method of putting the sections together protected all split-prone edges and also made the mats easy to roll up. The mats were put on the wigwam horizontally and overlapped like shingles.

Heavier bark, like elm, was cut in slabs two or three feet wide and six or seven feet long and flattened under weight. The slabs were then propped on end around the sides of the house and held in place either by withes encircling the house or by logs leaned against the walls. Elm-bark sides and a birch-bark roof were a good combination for a house, but no combination gave a very neat finish to the exterior.

The smoke hole, left open in the center of the roof, was protected by a square of bark which hung from one end of a long pole. This shield could be moved around as needed to keep the wind from blowing down the hole, or it could be used to cover the opening entirely in a deluge. The door was a hide curtain hung on the outside.

Inside the wigwam a fire burned in a shallow pit under the smoke hole. The floor was covered

33

with woven bulrush mats, and often the walls were also lined with decorated mats. Enclosing a rectangular space around the fire were platforms about a foot high, made of poles lashed together. They served as seats and beds. Still more mats were spread on the beds, and skins were piled thickly over them. Part of a wigwam interior shows in the illustration on page 26 in the preceding chapter.

In addition to the standard domed-type lodge, conical wigwams were used everywhere in the north. They had the advantage of being easily and quickly put up and were valuable as temporary shelters for hunting trips and other expeditions. The Penobscot in Maine used them exclusively in their later days before they moved into cottages, but their ancestors traditionally lived in domed lodges.

The frame of a conical wigwam was made of about a dozen long, straight poles. The first four of these were set up at the corners of a square about seven feet on a side for a small lodge, eleven or twelve feet for a large one. The poles leaned to the center and were tied together near their tops. The square was rounded to a circle by dispersing the rest of the poles among the first four. All of the pole tops were made fast. A ring of flexible withes, lashed inside the poles some three feet below their meeting point, added rigidity to the structure. The top of the doorway was made just above head height by a stick lashed between two poles. Covered with bark, and with a second set of poles to keep the bark in place, the house was finished. The covering wasn't carried quite to the top of the wigwam. This gave space for a smoke

Conical wigwam

hole and allowed the outside poles to be lashed to the inner ones. The door, hung on the outside of the opening, was of hide with a wooden batten fastened at top and bottom. The inside arrangement of a conical wigwam was similar to that of the standard kind.

The third kind of lodge, called *wigwassawigamig* by the Chippewa, is here called extended conical, because its ends were shaped like halves of the conical wigwam. The ends were joined at the top by a ridge pole about six feet long, against which side poles were leaned at the same angle as those of the ends. The covering and the method of anchoring it was identical to that of the conical type.

Lodges in these three shapes were common to most of the Algonquians, and all of them built smaller structures in similar forms for use as sweat houses and for other special purposes, such as making magic. A shaman (medicine man) would be bound hand and foot and left alone in a small hut. Strange noises and "spirit" conversations would be heard inside, the lodge would shake, and various articles would fly out of the smoke hole. When all was quiet again the shaman, found still in his bonds, would be ready and willing to prophesy. Sophisticated young Indians of recent times have amused themselves by building the shaman a lodge so rigid he couldn't shake it.

The Chippewa built very large lodges for the meetings of their secret society, the Midewiwin. These were enlargements and elongations of the domed kind of wigwam. The largest of them were thirty feet wide, half as high, and 200 feet long and could hold all the accredited members in the neighborhood.

Unfortunately, though the Algonquians were of one blood, they fought one another. Encroachments on hunting preserves, occasional woman-stealing, murder, or just pure devilment were excuse enough to start a neighborly war. So exposed villages were fortified; or if the population had to be widely scattered, a couple of strong points were set up to which the people could go in time of trouble.

An Indian fort was a simple stockade made of posts ten or twelve feet high set closely together. Our forefathers called them "castles." Most forts were circular, but some were square. A few had dry ditches around them. Small forts surrounded only a hut or two; large ones enclosed whole villages covering a couple of acres. A gate was too much of a problem for aboriginal ingenuity. Instead, they left one narrow opening, protected by a considerable overlap of the stockade walls, that could be barricaded.

Hunting

Though they didn't live exclusively on meat, game animals were of first importance to the woodland Indians. The major hunting season was from the beginning of February through April,

Wigwassawigamig

though deer and moose were shot or speared from canoes in the late fall. Each tribe had recognized hunting grounds that they would defend, and in some tribes these were subdivided so that each clan had its own area, marked with its totem cut on trees along the boundaries. The hunting grounds were frequently very far from the villages, and expeditions to them camped there for the whole season.

Temporary moosehide canoe

If possible, the journey to the hunting grounds was made by canoe, since that was by far the easiest way to bring out the meat and hides. If there was no convenient stream or if ice precluded canoeing, toboggans were dragged along by men on snowshoes. The Penobscot trekked into the woods on foot, and while there, built rough canoes covered with moosehide to float the meat out when the ice broke up in the spring.

Deer was the principal game everywhere in the woods. Bear ranged as widely. Moose was plentiful around the northern lakes, and caribou were once found much farther south than they are now. Small game wasn't passed up. Often it was con-

sidered a delicacy or offered something special in the way of fur; the beaver was valued on both counts. Muskrat, grouse, porcupine, rabbit, squirrel, otter, marten, and mink were all hunted or trapped in the woods.

The woodland Indians had large dogs around their camps. Sometimes they ate them and sometimes they made much of them as pets, but they didn't frequently use them for hunting. For one thing, a large dog was a nuisance in a canoe. However, there were other dogs, short-legged and rather short-nosed, which were fine in a canoe and were valuable for hunting any kind of burrowing animal. They'd go into a fox den or a beaver lodge and chase the animals out.

The main reasons for hunting in winter were that tracking was easy and that fast animals were slowed down by deep snow. Most of the hunting was done by clever stalking, approaching from down wind and getting to within sixty feet of the animal if possible without being detected. It was necessary to get that close to the quarry because the Indian bow didn't have a very long killing range; its maximum was about 125 feet, which, compared with the 220 yards of the English longbow, wasn't much.

35

Short-legged canoe dog
(a reconstruction)

Chippewa bow

Bows and Arrows

A Chippewa bow, unstrung, was a straight slat of wood about five feet long and about half an inch thick by two inches wide at its midpoint. Both thickness and width were tapered toward the ends, which were notched to retain the bowstring. Shagbark hickory, ash, white oak, and red cedar were the preferred woods in the East. The bow stave was split out of a log with wedges and cut and scraped to shape with beaver-tooth knives— a wearisome job.

Whenever an Indian found a likely piece of bow wood he took it home, removed the bark, and perhaps shaped it a little, roughly. Then he greased it, and hung it from the ceiling of the wigwam to season. From time to time it would be taken down and worked on, regreased, and put back. Though a bow would last for years, accidents could happen and it was wise to prepare for them. Bows in active service were cared for meticulously. They were unstrung and cased when not in use and were frequently oiled and rubbed to protect them from moisture. Boys worked at bowmaking from an early age and continued the craft all their lives. When a man became too old for hunting, he often became a professional bowyer or an arrow maker.

Most bowstrings were made of deer sinew or of fibers from the common nettle. Either kind was twisted together into a cord by rolling it with the hand against the thigh. A better bowstring than these could be made from the skin of a snapping turtle's neck. It was cut spirally into a long strip and then twisted. About as tough as any hide known to man, it would neither stretch nor shrink. Ordinarily, each end of the bowstring was tied to the bow with a clove hitch, but some tribes used a loop at one end that could be slipped into a notch when the bow was to be strung.

Among the forest-living Indians, arrows were made of wood. The viburnum bush had straight branches and was called arrowwood; dogwood shoots were also used because they tended to grow straight. When a shaft was not naturally straight, it was straightened with a drilled wood or bone tool. The arrow shaft, held straight by the lever-like tool, was heated over a fire until it would retain its new shape. (See illustration on page 102.)

Stone was used for arrowheads, but so was anything else that was sharp or could be sharpened. Horn, bone, shell, copper, and slate were used; so was the wood of the arrow shaft itself. In this case, the shaft was left thick at one end and either cut to a point or left blunt for bird shooting. As soon as the Indians began to get iron from the white men they abandoned all of the other materials for arrowheads and used it. As a rule, arrowheads were lashed on with sinew. The dried and separated strands were held in the mouth until they were thoroughly wet and flexible. Then they were tied around head and shaft under tension. When they shrank in drying they became very tight indeed.

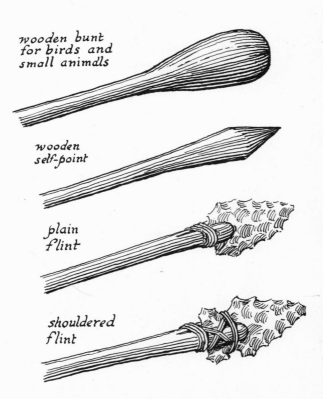

wooden bunt for birds and small animals

wooden self-point

plain flint

shouldered flint

Arrow points

Algonquian arrow

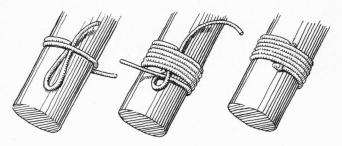

Three stages in lashing

The split feathers that fletched the arrow were lashed on the shaft with sinew, too, at both ends of the quill after the feathers had been glued in place with animal glue or with spruce gum. By holding the arrow under the left arm and rotating it with the left hand while the right held the sinew, a neat job could be done. First, a loop, made in one end of the sinew, was laid along the shaft. Then the long end of the sinew was wrapped over the loop toward its closed end. After a suf-

ficient number of turns, the sinew was passed through the loop and pinched firmly in place by pulling the short end.

Most arrows were fletched with three split feathers evenly spaced around the shaft, but arrows with only two feathers weren't unknown. Generally, they were put on parallel to the shaft, but sometimes they were given a spiral twist. Either was all right; the purpose of fletching an arrow is to slow up the butt a little and make the arrow fly straight. The split spines of the feathers usually lay against the shaft for their full length, but quite often they were sprung away from it slightly and were fastened only at their ends. The feathers were trimmed to three eighths of an inch or less in width. Ordinarily, they were five or six inches long, although some were much longer. The length of arrows themselves varied.

In the East, quivers were made of buckskin with a wooden stiffener or two in them. They hung upright behind the left shoulder from a baldric that passed over the right shoulder and under the left arm. Fastened to the quiver was the limp bow case, also of buckskin, and of course much longer than the quiver. Both articles were apt to be fringed and decorated.

It stands to reason that men who lived by the bow became proficient with it, so perhaps we should credit some of the unprovable tales of superhuman accomplishments, such as "mortar" shots (in which the arrow was shot upward and fell to strike its mark on the ground) and getting the last of ten arrows into the air before the first had landed.

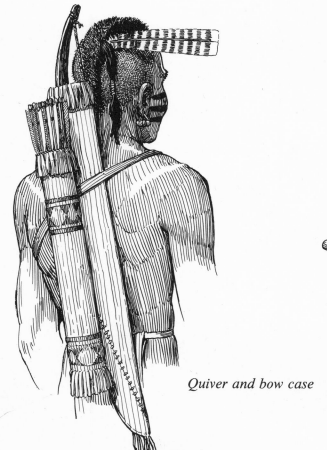

Quiver and bow case

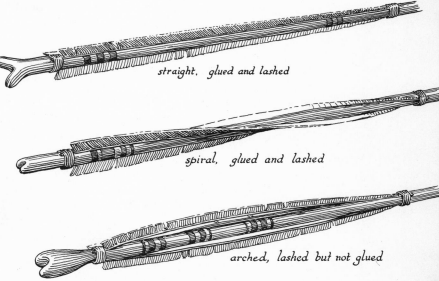

straight, glued and lashed

spiral, glued and lashed

arched, lashed but not glued

Fletching

Deadfall

Trapping and Woodsmanship

The Indians didn't hunt as sportsmen. They bagged game by any practical means. In addition to stalking and shooting, deadfalls were set for large animals, and snares for small ones. A deadfall was a heavy log, or several of them, supported at one end a couple of feet off the ground by a samson post to which bait was attached. The slightest touch would cause the post to slip out and the logs to drop. The simplest snare was a springy sapling, bent to the ground and held there by a thong attached to a delicately adjusted trigger on which bait was placed. A slip noose tied to the trigger line caught any animal that touched the bait.

The hunters thoroughly knew the habits of animals and took advantage of them. When deer gathered in protected "yards" in bad weather, they could be surrounded and slaughtered. When a cornered bear rose on its hind legs to attack, an Indian might suddenly toss it a spruce bough to hug. In the following instant of its helplessness, a stone ax crashed on its head.

It hardly needs to be said that these people knew the ways of the woods and could cope with nearly any situation in them, but there was never a woodsman so good that he couldn't get lost. A lost Indian would hole up where he was until he could see clearly and then decide which way he wanted to go. He could locate north by the sun or the polestar or, lacking both, he examined the trees, noting the moss on the north side of the trunks and the thicker growth of branches on the south. Then he would line up three trees in the direction he had elected to go and proceed to the second of the three. There he would line up his third tree with two more distant ones. As he continued to move forward, each tree added to his string was sighted from the side opposite to that from which the last sight had been taken. This compensated for the tree's thickness and overcame the tendency a human being has to walk a circle in the woods.

A man in the woods has to build a fire for comfort if not for survival. Indians had no matches or flint-and-steel, so getting an initial spark was the problem. It's true that fires were made by rubbing

Snare

two sticks together or by rotating a stick between the palms against a dry block of wood, but either way was slow, laborious, and uncertain. A bow drill was better and so was a pump drill, spun by unwinding a wrapped thong rapidly, but either was cumbersome to carry. The Indians used the pump drill, but no one has yet been able to determine positively that they didn't copy it from a European carpenter's tool.

The Indian woodsman's solution to the problem of getting fire was to carry a little of it with him. He lined a large shell with clay and filled it with powdery rotten wood; the best was yellow birch. A pea-sized ember started this spunk smoldering, and its nearly airtight case kept it burning slowly. The shell was carried in a bag and would keep fire all day.

Hunting areas had trails marked by simple blazes on trees. When an Indian left the trail, he marked his point of departure with a sloping stick that said, "I went this way." Two parallel sloping sticks meant, "I went this way toward my camp." A short stick standing upright at the lower end of

a sloping one meant, "I haven't gone far." At the high end, such a stick meant, "This is going to be a long trip." Several vertical sticks, each counting as one, indicated the expected days of absence.

Not all hunting was done in the woods, nor was all of it done away from home. Small animals and an occasional deer might be bagged near the village. Waterfowl were hunted on lakes and rivers and along the coast. The New England coastal Indians even put to sea for seal and porpoise. July was the time for seal. A pup shot then was fat enough to float.

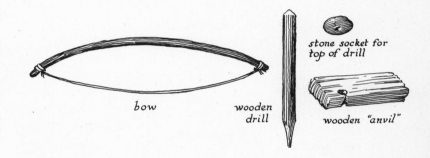

stone socket for top of drill

bow   *wooden drill*   *wooden "anvil"*

Fire-making machine. Similar ones were used at least as far back as the Basketmakers.

Making fire with a bow drill

New England Indians
night fishing

Fishing

Before the Europeans messed things up, salmon as heavy as forty pounds could be speared in New England rivers as soon as the lightning bugs began to flash. In the daytime a rock by a waterfall made a good platform for spearing. Still better was a canoe at night with a birch-bark torch on its bow, one man spearing and another paddling.

Shad ran early every spring in the Hudson, the Delaware, and the Susquehanna rivers and were taken in bark-fiber nets or on hooks. In the Great Lakes fish abounded, the largest being the sturgeon whose poundage ran into hundreds. Not to be despised, however, was the big pike called muskellunge by the Algonquins, the name it still bears.

Indians didn't disdain the lowly eel. In spring

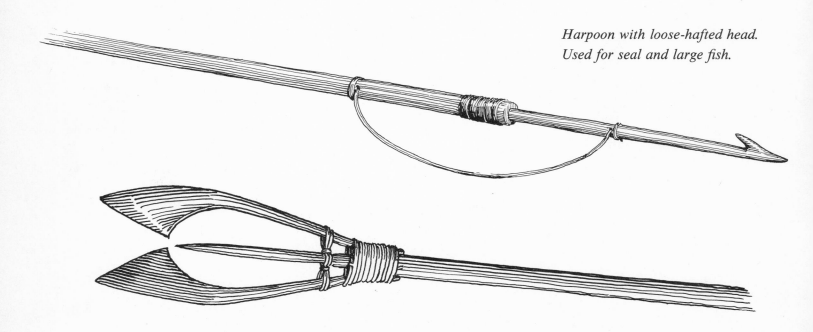

Harpoon with loose-hafted head.
Used for seal and large fish.

Wooden fish spear. The outer prongs are springy to grasp the fish.

when the eels' exodus to the sea began, they built weirs across streams, forcing the eels to pass through a narrow opening and over a kind of tray just below the surface of the water. It is difficult for eels to swim in such a shallow, and they—and fish, too—were taken in large quantities. It was the men's job to catch the eels. On the shore the women skinned and cleaned them and hung them over slow fires to smoke.

The Indians knew that pokeberries or jack-in-the-pulpit root mashed up and dumped into a slow stream will poison fish without making them inedible. When the dead fish floated to the top, children were sent into the water to gather them up. This the children hated; the poison irritated their skins.

Plenty of fish were caught on hooks, too. The wishbones of birds were doctored into fishhooks for bait fishing. Bone gorges were often used instead of hooks. A gorge was a straight piece of bone, less than an inch long and sharpened at both ends, with a line tied to its middle. Large fish would swallow a baited gorge whole. It went down end-on, but a jerk of the line turned it cross-wise, and the fish was caught.

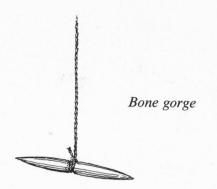

Bone gorge

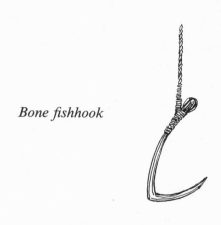

Bone fishhook

Camp at an eel weir

*Pounding corn
into meal*

Food and Cooking

There was no constant supply of fresh meat in an Indian village, but there was nearly always smoked meat—black and leathery—or smoked fish, and if one family had anything at all, everybody in the village got a little of it. Boys brought in a trickle of rabbits and birds. In some tribes shooting his breakfast was part of a boy's training—no game, no breakfast. There was apt to be a supply of corn on hand at most times, also dried squash; when these failed there were stores of nuts and of dried berries pressed into cakes.

Wherever fresh water was still and shallow, wild rice grew. It isn't really rice, but it's quite like it. It was a mainstay of the Great Lakes tribes but it was eaten all over the East. The Chippewa gathered it in canoes, striking the heads of the grass with sticks and shattering the grain onto mats spread in the bottom of the boat. To get ahead of the birds and to make sure that it wouldn't shatter of itself and be lost, wild rice was gathered just before it had fully ripened. Then it was spread out and dried before it was put into skin-lined pits and threshed by the men's stomping moccasins. The women winnowed it in bark trays and stored it in limp baskets shaped like bags. It was also put into birch-bark mocucks and stored underground, where it would keep for quite a while. Wild rice was good with duck or in venison stews. It still is!

There was no cane sugar and no honey; the English introduced bees. In the north and in the mountains, maple syrup and maple sugar served as sweetening instead. Indians gathered sap much as the whites later learned to gather it: Flat spiles, driven into gashes in the bark of the tree, conveyed the sap into birch-bark "buckets." The sap was boiled in troughs made of bark or wood and stored as syrup; or it was further boiled and poured into molds to crystallize as sugar. Maple syrup and water was a favorite drink. Some tribes are said to have fermented the syrup into a kind of beer, but it was never an extensive custom. The whole sap-gathering operation was the work of women and children. The maple groves, like the hunting grounds, were owned for generations by clans, never by individuals.

Cookery was simple, but some of it was good enough to be copied by the white men and to survive to the present day. It was done in the open whenever possible. Fresh meat was broiled on green sticks or boiled. The old criticism that the Indians burned meat on the outside and left the inside raw may have been made by someone who didn't care for rare meat. It's too late now to determine the right of that. Smoked meat was boiled, when it was cooked at all. Frying is said to have been done with raccoon fat on flat stones, but it's hard to be sure it wasn't an idea picked up from the white men.

Anciently, all of the Algonquians made clay pots, but the northern ones stopped fooling with them because it was so easy to fold a piece of birch bark into a container that would serve the same purpose. A birch-bark vessel could be used as a cooking pot. It served not only for boiling with hot stones dropped into the food, but it could also be hung over a fire for regular boiling. As long as it was full of liquid, it could even be set directly on

*Gathering maple sap
in a seamless birch-bark trough*

hot coals. Setting it on the coals was likely to ruin it for much further use, however. An Indian cooking fire was small; the butts of three sticks would make one.

A cooking vessel was hung over the fire at the end of a slanting pole that rested in a forked support and had its outer end held down by a stone. Or, occasionally, the pole rested horizontally across two forked posts, with the cooking utensils hung from it by wooden pothooks. A horizontal pole was used for indoor cooking in bad weather. The pole was then held up by the frame of the wigwam.

The summer camp was always made in a spot where gardening could be done. Tobacco was planted, and even the most dedicated hunters encouraged their wives to raise some corn, beans, and squash. These three were grown together in the same patch and were often cooked together in the same pot. The garden patch wasn't cleared. Trees in it were killed by girdling, and the vegetables were planted between them as they stood. Wherever corn was raised in the East, hominy was

an important food. It was made by boiling whole corn with wood ashes until the hulls loosened. The women picked off the hulls by hand and the naked grains were thoroughly washed to remove all traces of the lye from the ashes. They were boiled again before they were eaten. Beans, fat, and any leftover bones went into the pot with them. A good bone could be cooked several times over in batches of hominy. Corn meal, which was fine, and samp, which was coarse but not as coarse as hominy, were made by pounding precooked kernels of corn in a mortar or between two stones, the lower one resting on a piece of bark to catch

Chippewas gathering wild rice

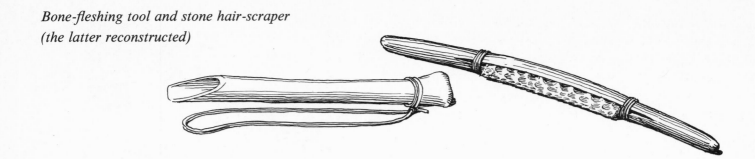

the product. Both samp and meal were boiled; but corn meal was sometimes made into cakes and cooked on flat stones, tilted up to the fire, or put between two large leaves and cooked in the ashes. These two methods and some cooking that was done in covered pits were as near as the Indians ever came to baking.

Ordinarily, there was but one meal a day in an Indian household. This was eaten about the middle of the morning, but anyone was at liberty to help himself whenever he was hungry. When the master of the house or any visitor entered, food was put before him at once. Bowls for food were made from maple burls, which were already round on the outside and which, because of their tortuous grain, didn't split easily. The hollowing of a bowl was done by burning and scraping. Food trays were made of wood and so were ladles and spoons, though bark versions of all these things were also used.

Tannery

The extensive use of hides by Indians is well-known; the skins of animals were, in fact, nearly as valuable as their flesh. Since the hides had varying characteristics, each had its appropriate uses. Tanning of hides was done entirely by women. Every lodge had the necessary "horse" and frame. The horse was a six-foot log with its bark removed. One end rested on the ground; the other was raised about thirty inches high on a pair of angled legs. A fresh deerhide, hair-side down, was thrown over the horse and was scraped to remove all of the flesh, fat, and membrane that still clung to it. The tool used was the shinbone of a deer, cut to a long, slanting blade. Gripped palm down, the blade was on the little-finger side of the hand and the scraping motion was away from the worker.

The cleaned hide was thoroughly washed and left to soak in water for three days; then it was wrung out and put back on the horse hair-side up. The soaking loosened the hair enough so that it could be removed by scraping. The job was laborious, because not only the hair but the top layer of skin was taken off. The scraper was pushed against the grain of the hair.

The next step in tanning was "braining," to cure and soften the hide. Brains of large animals were dried and stored for this use. When they were needed, they were stewed with a little fat and then thoroughly rubbed into both sides of

Fleshing a hide

the damp hide. The skin was sprinkled, rolled up tightly, and left overnight to absorb its braining. Next day the tanner wrung the hide out thoroughly by passing it around a small tree and twisting it this way and that with a three-foot stick.

Then the hide was put on the stretching frame. A couple of saplings, growing about seven feet apart, served as uprights. Two poles were lashed across them, one a foot or so from the ground and one as much higher as it needed to be. Holes were made all the way around the hide and it was laced to the frame by strips of bark fiber run through holes. The lacings were pulled as tight as possible and slackness was taken up as it appeared.

The next step was "beaming." It stretched and softened the hide and it was hard work. The woman forcibly rubbed the whole surface with a long-handled tool that had a working end of stone or horn set at a right angle. When beaming was finished, the leather was dry, pliable, and nearly white. There remained only smoking to finish the job. The hide was temporarily shaped into a

Wringing

cylindrical bag and inverted over a smudge fire of green or rotten wood. After a time the bag was turned inside out to smoke the other side. Ten minutes was enough for smoking a thin hide; a thick one might take an hour. The finished color varied with the duration of smoking and the kind of wood used. Grays could be obtained; but most hides ran from cream to tan to quite dark brown.

Beaming

Cape sleeves

Clothing

The day-to-day clothes of the Indians were the minimum that would serve the purpose. Children began to dress like adults when they were ten years old. Until then, they wore nothing except moccasins, and in cold weather, robes. Little sewing was done on any Indian garments because sewing leather is laborious, requiring holes punched with an awl for each stitch. Skins were cut so they could be worn conveniently, but they were not really tailored to fit. Excess ends and edges were often slashed into fringe.

Most Northeastern women wore a knee- or calf-length skirt that was simply a squared-up skin wrapped around the waist and held there by a belt. The skirt barely overlapped on the left side, allowing the thigh to be readily bared for rolling fibers against it to make twine. They wore moccasins and knee-high leggings when they were needed. The upper garment was ordinarily nothing, but when weather demanded it, they put on a skin with a hole in it, worn poncho-fashion. A robe was added in real cold weather.

Northern Algonquian women wore a kind of dress made of two skins, hung from the shoulders front and back and belted at the waist. Over this in cool weather they wore a pair of cape sleeves. These were joined at the back of the neck and caught together by a strip across the chest. They were sewn at the wrists but otherwise were entirely open. It's said that Chippewa women wore an underskirt woven from nettle fiber, but this sounds suspiciously like the white woman's sophistication. Some kind of necklace made of shells or claws, of deer hoofs or of bones was usually worn, and ear ornaments were customary, at least on state occasions. They wore their hair long in one or two braids.

The men wore far less, even in cold weather, than most white men could make out with. In summer their only clothing was a breechclout and, perhaps, moccasins. A breechclout was a narrow strip of leather, three or four feet long, passed between the legs and brought upward under a belt; the ends hung down over the belt, front and back. One end was sometimes fringed and decorated with a little porcupine quillwork. Leggings were needed in woods. Sometimes they reached to just below the knee and were held up by bands tied around the legs. More often they reached well up the thigh and were suspended by a strip of leather from the belt. Even the long ones often had garters below the knees. Algonquian leggings weren't sewn into tubes like trousers; they were merely tied together with strips of hide at half a dozen points down the outside of the leg. They were quite tight and didn't have long fringes that would catch in bushes.

In winter men sometimes wore a kind of chasuble made of two skins, with or without fur, caught together on the shoulders; but usually a fur robe or a leather or rabbitskin blanket was

Moosehide boot

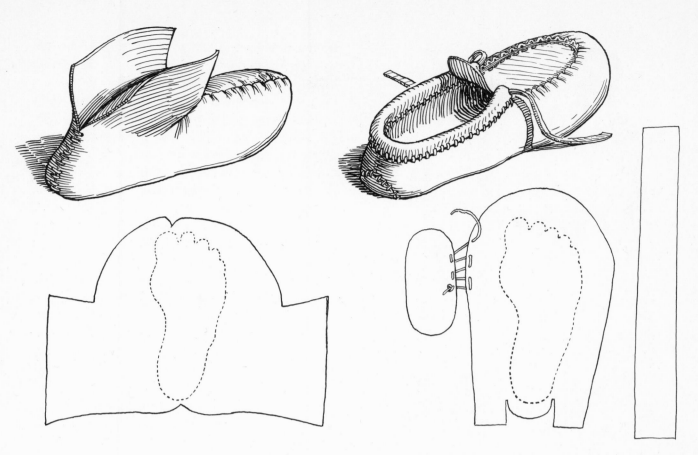

One-piece and three-piece moccasins and their patterns

enough. Where the frost really crackled, they wore clumsy moosehide boots with the hair on the outside, probably over moccasins. These boots were made from a section of the skin of the animal's hind leg, taken just where the hock bends, so that the heel of the boot came ready-made. Ordinary moccasins were stuffed with deer hair or cattail fluff to make them warmer in winter.

Two kinds of moccasins were used in the woods; both were soft and without added soles. The simpler, and probably the older kind, was made of a single piece of buckskin or moosehide. A seam up the back and another from the toe up the middle of the instep were all the sewing needed. The front seam was puckered a little to shape the shoe and was ordinarily covered with quillwork. In cutting the pattern enough extra leather was allowed to make a generous cuff at the ankle around which a string could be tied. The cuff was worn either turned down or standing up. One large buckskin made nine pairs of men's moccasins.

The other kind of moccasin was made quite differently, of three separate pieces. The body of the moccasin was sewed to a U-shaped vamp which covered the top of the foot. The vamp lay flat but the larger piece had to be strongly puckered between stitches to make the two fit together. This gave the shoe what we usually think of as the moccasin shape: a soft sole rounding up over the toe and sides. The third piece was a simple tube of hide sewn around the top of the shoe with its ends open at the front so that a drawstring could be run in it.

Moccasins for children and old people were similar in shape to the one-piece kind. They were made of scrap leather and had a seam not only on top of the foot but also the full length of the sole. Children's moccasins frequently had holes in the soles. This was so that evil spirits, seeing their footgear was unfit for travel, wouldn't kidnap them.

Woodland men wore their hair in several different ways depending on their tribe and their personal taste. Some wore it full length in two braids or unbraided and bound into a couple of hanks; others affected the roach cut. Most of the head was plucked or singed bare for a roach cut; only a strip of hair was left from front to back.

The strip was a couple of inches wide and not so neatly cut as a modern barber could do it. The scalp lock was left long at the crown of the head in the middle of the roach. Presumably this was for the convenience of enemies, giving them a good handhold when they wished to separate the owner from his headpiece. Sometimes the scalp lock hung loose or merely had a string tied around it for comfort; sometimes it was braided; and sometimes it was tightly wrapped for two thirds of its length and stood straight up, the free hair at the top splaying over like a small parasol.

A hint at the texture of a rabbit-skin blanket

Eastern Indians didn't go in for feathers as heavily as the Plainsmen did. A man of acknowledged bravery might wear one feather at whatever angle it pleased him. A man who had been severely wounded in battle could wear a feather with a split quill. There was no accumulation of feathers, each awarded for an achievement, as in the West.

The most usual ceremonial headdress in the East was the artificial roach. It was made of stiff hair from moose, deer, or porcupine. The hair was much longer than that of the roach cut, and the crest it made from front to back was narrow. These roaches were dyed red as a rule. An artificial roach was kept on by tying it to the scalp lock which was pulled up through a hole in the roach base.

Women wore nothing whatever on their heads except when the weather forced them to do so. In winter, crude fur caps of unknown shape were worn by both men and women; or sometimes the whole skin of a fox or an otter was tied around the head, leaving the crown exposed. This was the origin of the frontiersman's raccoon cap.

His robe served the Indian as overcoat and bed covering. It was about six feet square as a rule. The lightest ones were made of dressed buckskin; the heaviest were bearskin with the fur left on. Skins were sewed together as needed, and practically all fur-bearing animals contributed.

There were Indians in the West who knew how to weave cloth blankets, but twined rabbit-skin blankets were woven by the Easterners and almost all other Indians. Such blankets were light and warm. They had a fur surface on both sides and they were nearly wind- and waterproof. Strips of rabbit skin, cut spirally so they were quite long, were twisted into a soft cord and used for both warp and weft. In weaving, the warp hung loose from a horizontal pole like very long fringe. Two strands of weft were carried across the warp together and were crossed in each space between the warps to enclose them. It was slow work.

Most rabbit blankets were twined so loosely that a finger could be put through them anywhere. Because of this the warp and weft had to be tied together where they crossed. A six-foot blanket required from 100 to 200 rabbit skins, depending on the closeness of the weave.

Cradleboards

Babies wore cradleboards. They were bandaged into them when they were but a few days old and kept there most of the time until they were ready to walk. They could do none of the kicking and squirming that is considered good for modern babies, though their efforts to kick against resistance may have provided exercise. Indian babies were not only comfortable and cheerful in their strait jackets, but they clamored to be put into them when they were tired. Soft moss and cattail down, both well dried, were put in with them to add to their comfort and to provide an absorbent, disposable diaper.

Algonquian cradleboards were carefully made of wood and hide. A small shelf at the bottom supported the child's feet, and a wooden bow projected from the top. The bow supported a drapery that protected the baby's head from sun and insects. Bird skulls or other small objects hung

Cradleboard

done on birch bark, the ends of each quill were put through holes in the bark and bent inward on the back, like a paper staple. Lining the underside was all that was needed to keep the work in place.

Finished quillwork is shiny. The surface looks a little like straw, but more dense. The material can be used to produce curved lines of openwork, a favored method in the East, or the quills can be placed side by side to cover whole areas solidly, as was preferred in the West. Much of the work was done on buckskin, and quill ornaments, such as strips for covering moccasin seams, were transferred to new articles when the old ones wore out.

On buckskin the quills were bent and sewn on, the stitches being concealed entirely, because they held only the bent-under part. For narrow lines a flattened quill was wrapped spirally around each stitch; for flat bands the wrapping was across two lines of stitches. There were variations; for instance, a quill could be laced back and forth between two lines of stitches to give a zigzag effect, or two quills could be interlaced as a braided

from the bow to amuse the occupant. The board was padded and the baby's head was not bound to it, as was the practice in some other areas, so it was not flattened. The wide doeskin band by which the baby was laced in was decorated with embroidery or with porcupine quillwork. A leather strap fastened at the junction of bow and board was used to hang the cradle on a convenient peg or as a carrying strap across the mother's forehead when the baby was on her back.

Quillwork

Long before they ever saw the white man's small glass beads the Indians decorated their clothing and accessories with porcupine quills. Porcupines were found all over this continent except in the Arctic. Their quills are scattered thickly through their fur. An adult porcupine has about 30,000 of them; hollow, white for most of their length but with dark-brown tips. They are loosely attached and will come free at a touch.

Indian women soaked the quills to soften them and quite often they dyed them. When she was working, a woman held a few quills in her mouth to soften them further and flattened each one with her teeth before she applied it. If the work was

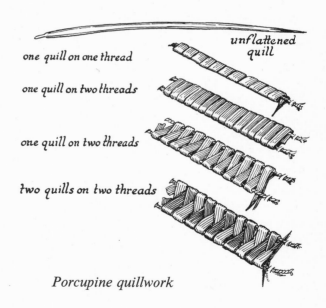

one quill on one thread

unflattened quill

one quill on two threads

one quill on two threads

two quills on two threads

Porcupine quillwork

pattern. Quills were also wrapped around pipestems and on the units of fringe.

The finest quillwork was done by the Canadian Athapascans, and the Algonquians may have learned the craft from them. Algonquian designs tended to be based on a double-curve motif, which made it very easy for them to adopt scroll and

49

floral designs from the Europeans. They did this so enthusiastically that it's now hard to say what is truly original with them; but it's doubtful that the old work ever made use of flowers as newer work does.

Cordage

The Indians had much need of thread, string, and twine. They made these things from whatever materials they could find. Tough spruce and larch rootlets were used for special purposes but by far the commonest material in the woods was basswood bark. Any tree with a fibrous inner bark is called basswood. In the North it was the American linden, in the South the tulip poplar. Other barks were also used.

Bark was taken from young trees and softened in water for a couple of weeks, so that full-length strips an inch or so wide could be pulled off the inner side, layer after layer of them, down to the useless outer bark. The strips were rolled up and left to dry until they were needed. They became brittle and it was necessary to moisten them before they were used.

For casual tying, nothing more needed to be done to the bark, but for such uses as net twine and rope, the bark was boiled an hour or two with

Twisting basswood bark

wood ashes to make it stronger. Then it was further split and softened by pulling it back and forth through a hole made in a bone or by hand-working. The wet fiber was twisted by rolling it against the bare thigh. A single strand was rolled with a downward motion; when two strands were twisted together, the motion was reversed. New strands were spliced in as needed and cords of great length were made.

Fine thread was made from the fibers of the false nettle, a tall weed with a reedlike stalk. The stalks were rotted under water and then beaten to get the fibers out. The result was long white thread of considerable strength that could be twisted together just as bark fiber was twisted. Nettle thread was used for sewing, for making fine-meshed nets, and for snares. Small bags were sometimes woven from it by the twining method.

Snowshoes

Since snowshoes were used for walking, the lightest possible construction was wanted. Hunting snowshoes for men were over three feet long and quite narrow, with toes that turned up slightly. The frame was ash, cut green and bent to shape by heating over a fire. Ordinarily a single piece made the entire frame, rounded at the toe and pointed at the back where the ends were lashed together.

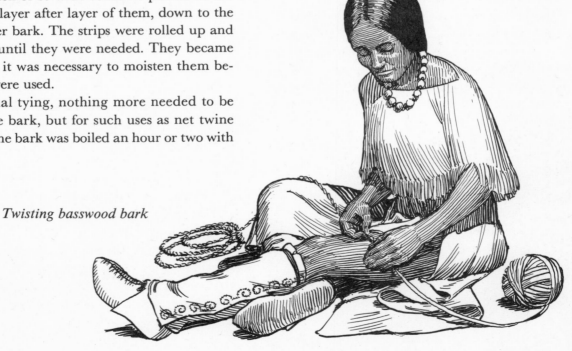

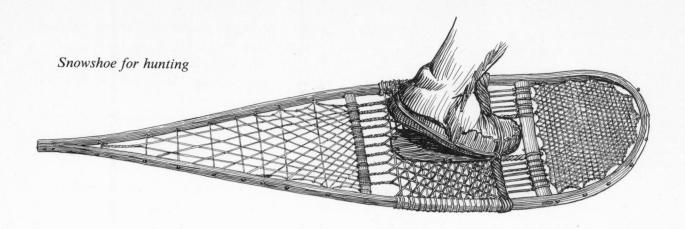

Snowshoe for hunting

Wooden thwarts were placed across the frame with their ends inserted into it. Most snowshoes had two thwarts. One just ahead of the wearer's toe, eight or ten inches from the front of the snowshoe; the other some twelve inches behind the first. A close-meshed netting of light sinew filled in the space between the toe of the snowshoe and the first thwart. The strands of this netting were anchored in holes in the frame and the thwart.

A couple of inches back of the front thwart and parallel to it, a thick cord made of many strips of rawhide was strung across the snowshoe. This took the weight of the wearer's foot in walking, and the opening between it and the thwart allowed the toe of his moccasin to pass downward through the snowshoe as his heel lifted. A thong was caught to the thick cord and was bound over the toe of the wearer's moccasin and around the back of it in such a way as to keep the snowshoe on and yet allow his heel to be raised freely.

The midsection of the snowshoe, between the thick cord and the back thwart, was crisscrossed by a web of stout rawhide strips wrapped *over* the frame and over the back thwart. Actually, the foot cord was above this web and was partly

supported by it, since some of the web's strips were brought straight forward on either side of the wearer's foot and were passed around the front thwart. There was a rawhide pad on the web for the foot to rest on. The coarse-meshed netting that filled in the heel of the snowshoe was passed through holes in the frame.

Women and children used "bear-paw" snowshoes. A woman's shoes were a bit less than a foot wide and about a foot and a half long. They were roughly egg shaped and the more pointed end was the front. Bear-paw snowshoes were crudely made. The frames were often crooked. They had two thwarts also, but all the spaces were filled in with coarse twined weaving, very open, and all of the strands were laced over the frame.

Mats, Bags, and Baskets

Mats and bags were an important part of woodland housekeeping and much bark fiber went into their making. Cedar-bark mats for the beds and floor of the wigwam were made with a straight basket weave, the same material being used for both warp and weft. The warp strips were hung on a horizontal pole. Weaving was done without a shuttle; alternate warps were picked up by hand, probably several at a time, and the weft was passed under them.

Rush mats were made in a similar way except that rushes were used for the warp only. The weft was basswood fiber, woven in either a straight basket weave, like the cedar mats, or with a twined weave, in which case the pairs of twisted wefts were carried across the mat an inch or so apart.

Cattail-reed mats for house sheathing were not woven. The reeds were hung from a pole and

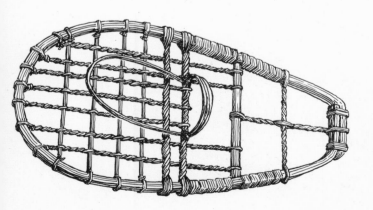

Woman's bear-paw snowshoe

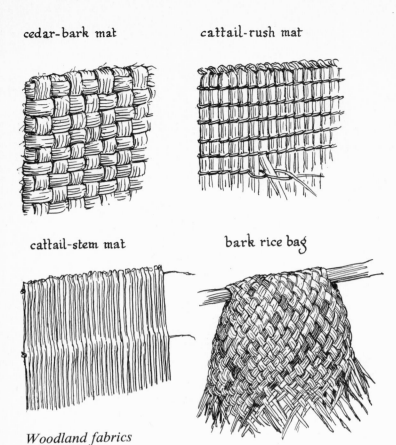

cedar-bark mat   cattail-rush mat

cattail-stem mat   bark rice bag

Woodland fabrics

strips of basswood fiber were sewn through them, piercing them in lines about eight inches apart. The reeds were laid as close together as possible and sometimes were lapped over each other to gain thickness.

Cedar bark and basswood were also used to make storage bags; some of these were twined, others were plaited. In either case the strands were laid across a pole so that the ends hung down equally on both sides of it. The work proceeded clear around the bag, so that there were no seams in it except those closing the two holes where the pole passed through. All the strands in a plaited bag served as both warp and weft and the resulting weave was diagonal. Any one strand in a bag could be traced spirally around it.

The Indians also used plaiting for belts and to make headbands for carrying burdens. Such a band, with carrying ropes at each end, is known as a tumpline. The band rested on the carrier's forehead; the ropes were secured around the burden, some part of the weight of which was taken by the bearer's back.

The tribes that had birch bark tended to neglect basket making and none of the Easterners were really good at it. Hemispherical baskets were made of peeled willow. Flexible twigs, soaked to make them more so, were woven on a somewhat stiffer frame of withes arranged like the spokes of a wheel at the bottom center of the basket. Extra spokes were added as the original ones spread too far apart. Baskets were also plaited from black-ash splints obtained by pounding a log until strips of its wood were loosened enough to be pulled off.

Birch Bark

Birch trees grew everywhere north of Manhattan Island and were used to some extent by all the Indians in the area. Few large trees grew south of Lake Erie, however, so it was the northerners who were really skillful in handling the bark. Birch bark is remarkable stuff. It is wind- and waterproof and highly resistant to decay. It isn't without fault, however. It's made up of many layers of paperlike thinness and when it dries out thoroughly they tend to separate. It also has a tendency to split crosswise, so the edges must always be secured and stitches taken in it staggered in length in order to hold. Winter bark, removed from the trees in spring, is the strongest and most durable.

Birch bark is resinous. Dried and rolled, it made fine flaring torches to light the camp at need. It is pliable, and in Indian hands it was versatile. It could be folded into a drinking cup in an instant, used to splint a broken leg, or to shroud the dead. Heating the bark made it take a sharp bend more readily, and this method was usually used in mak-

A plaited tumpline

Birch-bark utensils. A mocuck and its lid, a ladle, and a seamless cooking tray.

ing the variety of utensils for which it served. The leak-proof troughs in which maple sap was cooked were made from a single piece of birch bark, the ends being creased into shape so that there were no seams.

By far the commonest birch-bark container was the mocuck, with a square bottom larger than its round top, that served as box or basket at need. It was made in all sizes, the larger ones being stiffened with willow struts. Mocucks weren't seamless, like the troughs, but were cut from a pattern and sewed together with basswood fiber. The white outer surface of the bark was turned to the

inside of the mocuck; the outside showed the rosy tan of the inner bark. The top edge was bound to a willow or ash splint that reinforced it and kept the bark from splitting. The seams were often covered with pine pitch to keep moisture out, and most mocucks had lids.

Birch-bark Canoes

There were tribal variations in the design and the methods of construction of birch-bark canoes, but basically all of them were much alike. The most obvious differences were in the shapes of the

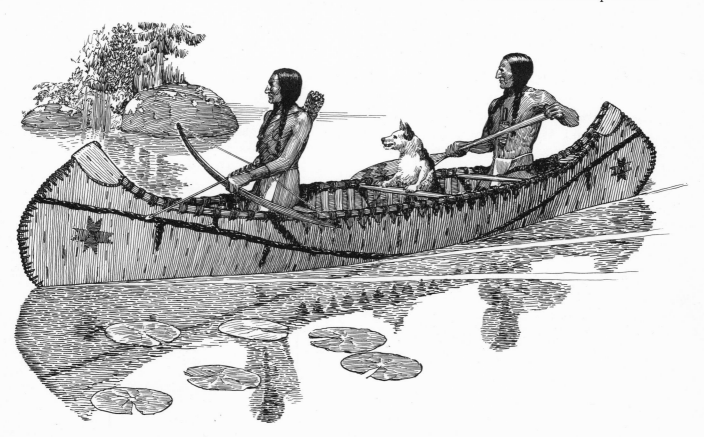

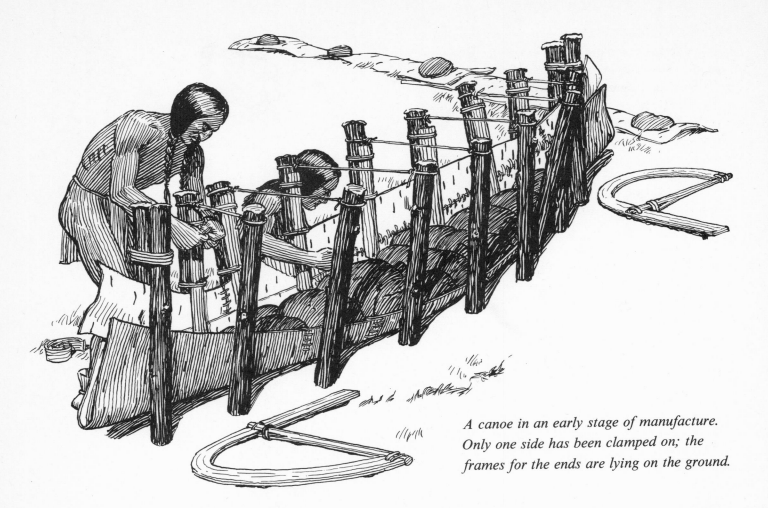

A canoe in an early stage of manufacture. Only one side has been clamped on; the frames for the ends are lying on the ground.

upturned ends. In Maine canoes were turned up but slightly. This is the shape the white man has copied in canvas and sheet metal. On the western Great Lakes the Chippewa curved the bow and stern up and back, rather high, to make what was perhaps the handsomest of all canoes.

Building a canoe was a joint project for two men and four women that might take from ten days to three weeks. The first chore was assembling material. While the women dug and prepared spruce and tamarack roots for sewing the seams and gum for caulking them, the men collected and shaped the heavier stuff.

The best and most commonly used wood for the ribs and planking was arbor vitae, sometimes called white cedar. It was light, straight-grained and strong. The men cut what they needed, split it with wedges, and trimmed up the pieces with crooked knives. The wood was given its final shape while it was still green and was stored under water until it was needed.

Large sheets of winter bark were required and birch trees had to be felled to get them. Canoes

may once have been made from the skin of a single tree but birch trees haven't come that large for a long time. Lacking a giant birch, the Indians used three pieces, one for the bottom and two for the sides, measuring the full length of the boat. The bark was kept moist and pliable throughout the construction of the canoe.

A level spot in the shade was made smooth as a work place and two rows of posts were driven into it, marking out a crib that would contain the finished craft exactly. The piece of bark for the bottom was put into this crib with its white side up. The tan inner surface showed on the outside of the canoe. Since the bark curled naturally the other way, it had to be held down with large stones. This bottom piece lay almost flat amidships, but its edges sloped upward in long sweeps toward the tapering ends at bow and stern.

The side pieces were cut to shape; deep in the middle to reach the edge of the bottom piece, narrow near the ends, and then flaring wide again to provide for the high bow and stern. This was hard to do, and the bark was gored and sewn with

54

spruce rootlets to make it take its proper shape. The side pieces were clamped into place with temporary slats, lashed to the tops of the crib posts.

Then the women went to work; first gluing the overlaps with spruce gum that had been thickened by boiling, then sewing the long seams with long-and-short stitches. The holes for each stitch were made with a bone awl. After the ends of the canoe were cut to shape and sewn, bent struts were thrust into them to hold them rigid. The top edges of the bark along both sides of the boat were sewn to narrow, inside rails that met at both ends and were lashed together there. Ancient canoe makers may have rolled the bark around these rails.

At this point there stood in the stocks a bark bag in the complete shape of a canoe. The next step was to stuff the planking and ribs into it. Ribs were bent in advance. Each one was about two inches wide and three eighths of an inch thick. Different makers spaced ribs from two inches to

Sewing the bow

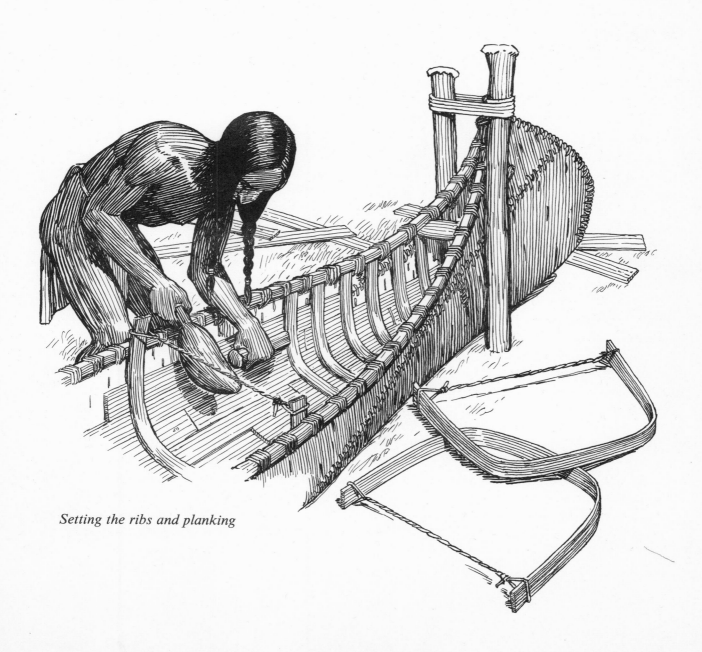

Setting the ribs and planking

as much as four inches apart. The planks were very thin, less than a quarter of an inch. They were between two and three inches wide and four or five feet long. The edges of some of them had to be tapered to make them fit.

The work was begun at one end of the canoe, and as stones and clamps were removed the ribs and planks were put in together. The planks lay next to the bark and were held there by the ribs, which were hammered in over them with a wooden mallet. A square-ended tool was used with the mallet for settling both ribs and planks into place. The ends of the ribs were forced under the top rails and were held there by their own springiness. Planking covered the whole bottom and lower sides of the canoe but didn't reach the gunwale by several inches.

Next, five carefully measured thwarts were cut and put in. The longest was amidships; the two shortest, which were wider than the others, went near the ends; and the other two were placed at the quarters. The ends of the thwarts were lashed to the rails and an outside gunwale was put on over the lashings. It is doubtful that the ancient canoes had a capping rail and the Algonquians are said to have used no gunwale.

The entire canoe had been kept damp all this time. It was now straightened by brute strength, where it needed it, and lashed tightly to the crib posts to dry straight. The last operation was to lift the boat out of its stocks, turn it over, and pay all the seams with thick spruce gum mixed with charcoal and fried in grease. This is what makes the rough black lines on the outside of a birch-bark canoe.

An ordinary canoe eighteen feet long could easily be carried by one man. Two men could carry the largest ones, up to forty feet long, that needed ten paddlers. By way of equipment a canoe had a birch-bark bailer; a puncture-mending kit, containing a bit of birch bark, some spruce root, and some pine gum; an anchor, which was a hefty stone with a groove pecked around its middle for a line; and a ten-foot pole for fending off snags in rapids. Birch bark is fragile. In rocky water a temporary sheathing of spruce bark was tied around a boat to protect it.

Paddlers in a one- or two-man canoe usually knelt in the bottom on a folded fawn skin instead of sitting on a thwart. Most paddles were spruce but a few uncomfortably heavy ones were maple. They were the same size as modern paddles, six feet long for the stern and five for the bow, and they were the same general shape, except that the shaft tapered from the upper grip to the blade instead of being straight with a knob head.

Sports and Games

All Indians were keen on competitive games and nearly all of their games involved gambling. They would bet all they had, and sometimes a finger to boot, on the outcome of a contest or on their ability to guess which moccasin hid a pebble. The winner of a finger was entitled to wear it as an ornament; necklaces were sometimes made of them.

The games described here were not the only ones the woodland Indians played; these are the ones that appear to have originated with them or to have been more popular with them than with tribes elsewhere.

Snowsnake was played by all the northern tribes on a level track made by dragging a log or a boy through the snow. The "snakes" were made of maple. They were quite long and about an inch and a half thick at the head, which was turned up slightly. The stick itself was made very smooth and tapered toward the tail, which ended in a notch for the thrower's finger.

The head of the snowsnake was carved into some semblance of a real snake's head. A handy way of ornamenting the body of the snake was to remove part of the bark in a pattern, often a sim-

56

Snowsnake

ple spiral, then to smoke the whole stick before taking off the rest of the bark. The wood under this bark was unsmoked, of course, and therefore light in color.

The game's object was to slide the snowsnake down the course as far as possible. The throw was commonly, but not always, underhand, and a good man could send his snake rattling down a slippery track to notable distances. Encouraging speeches and songs were addressed to the snake before throwing—"Baby needs a new pair of moccasins!" The distance of each throw was marked by sticking the snake upright in the snow beside the place where it stopped sliding. The winner took all the snakes. There were also side bets.

The moccasin game was probably played by more woodland Indians than any other sitting-down game. Two teams of three men each played it to the accompaniment of drumming and singing and there was usually a large audience. A game might last several days, or until one team had lost everything except its breechclouts.

The game was played with four moccasins and four small objects that were identical except that one was inconspicuously marked. The objects might be pebbles, foot bones, or fruit pits; in later days they were lead bullets. The play was a matter of taking turns at guessing under which moccasin the opposing team had put the marked piece. The guess, accompanied by the tense excitement of the spectators, was indicated with a three-foot rod. Score was kept with wooden tallies.

The moccasin game

The Council

4

The Iroquois

There weren't more than thirty thousand of them when they were at the height of their power. They were surrounded on all sides by enemy Indians whom they subjugated. They made their weight felt northward into Canada, as far south as North Carolina, as far east as Maine, and as far west as the Mississippi. They were able to do this because they were fierce and implacable warriors and because they had the only organized government north of Mexico. It's true, however, that they reached their ultimate dominance by being the first Indians to get hold of firearms.

Their Algonquian neighbors called them, among less complimentary names, *Irinakoiw*—"real adders"—and the French turned the word into Iroquois. They called themselves *Hodenosaunee*, "The People of the Longhouse." They were known to the English as the Five Nations because of the five tribes (later there were six) of which their League was composed. The five were spread in a long band across what is now northern New York. Reading from east to west, they were the Mohawk, the Oneida, the Onandaga, the Cayuga, and the Seneca. Some of them are still there. There were other Iroquoian tribes outside the Five Nations; the Hurons and the Erie are examples. It's usually said that the origins of the Iroquois were in the South, and it's true that they recognized kinship with some Southern tribes, but archaeological findings indicate the possibility that both they and the Southern tribes had a common origin in the Mound Builders along the Ohio River.

The language of the Five Nations had the peculiarity of using no sounds made with the lips. If they had used letters, there would have been no *b, p,* or *m.* Since there was no *f, l,* or *v* either, Iroquois speech had a windy sound. Someone has said that it was ideal for talking with a pipe in one's teeth.

The Clans

Many American Indian tribes lived according to some variation of the clan system of social organization, but since none observed it more rigidly than the Iroquois, they make a good example. The principal aims of the system were to prevent inbreeding and to arrange for inheritance.

Clan totems have been mentioned. These were the symbols adopted by the clans and the names of the totem animals were also the names of the clans. A clan was actually an enormous family, related largely by edict, but nevertheless descended from a common ancestor. The Iroquois counted eight clans and each of the Five Nations had all eight.

Originally, by Iroquois legend, there were but two clans, the Wolf and the Deer. Whether man or woman, a Wolf could marry only a Deer; and a Deer could marry only a Wolf. Actually, of course, an individual was as closely related to the opposite clan as he was to his own. Later the clans

became so big they were divided. From the Wolf came the Bear, the Beaver, and the Turtle; from the Deer came the Snipe, the Heron, and the Hawk. The eight clans thus formed two groups; anthropologists call them moieties. The marriage taboo persisted and no one might marry into a clan of his own group.

When a man married he left his home and went to live with his wife's family, but he didn't become a member of his wife's clan. His children, however, did belong to her clan. Clan relationship was carried so far that a father, though regarded with affection, wasn't thought of as a relative at all, and a son felt no responsibility to care for him in his old age. "Let him go to his own people," he would say. And the father did, and they took him in. Clan membership was felt so strongly that a family would receive a complete stranger as a brother if he was of their totem. Inheritance was entirely through the mother. She owned all of the family's goods. The system had its merits, especially among the Iroquois where all the husbands of sisters were regarded as being married to all of the sisters. A father wasn't an altogether certain thing; a mother was.

There were some peculiar side effects to this system. A man had no responsibility for training his own sons. That was the job of his brothers-in-law. His interest was in the education of his sister's sons. A sachemship in the League Council was

Iroquois women processing corn.
At center, the grains are shelled
from the cobs;
at right, they are boiled;
at left, they are ground
in a mortar.

hereditary in the clan of the sachem. The sachem's sons therefore were not in line of succession, but his brothers and nephews were.

Marriages were arranged by mothers. Among other Indian tribes a young man could choose his girl and make a bid for her, but not among the Iroquois. In their wisdom, the mothers usually married off a twenty-five-year-old warrior to an experienced widow of forty, and a twenty-year-old girl got a widower of sixty! This was ancient practice and was modified later.

The League

Indians didn't worry at all about recording their history for posterity. Nothing would be known of the workings of the League of the Iroquois if white men hadn't written about it. The date of its beginning isn't known; the earliest estimated date is 1450, the latest 1570, with most modern opinion favoring the later one. It was founded by the efforts of a single man, an Onandaga named Dagonoweda, who is also called Hiawatha. The League was forged complete at a "constitutional convention" that lasted for days. It's claimed that the original plan was never changed very much.

The five tribes had been battling one another, but Dagonoweda persuaded them to set up a common government with a system of representation. His proclaimed idea was to expand the League indefinitely; to take in any and all tribes and abolish war altogether. Perhaps there should be a statue of him in front of the United Nations buildings. What he succeeded in doing was uniting his own people and making them the strongest group in North America.

The government of the League was in the hands of forty-eight men who are now spoken of as sachems, though the word is Algonquian, not Iroquois. All of the sachemships were supposed to be equal but in actual practice some seem to have been more powerful than others. A sachem had not only a voice in the Council of the League, but also full personal authority in his own nation and in any of the other four.

Meetings of the Council were called by sending a belt of wampum to each sachem. The meetings were not private; in fact, everybody who could possibly do so attended them. There was much

oratory. Questions were proposed for acceptance or rejection, but there was no vote. Each of the four classes of sachems met and determined a position; then the spokesmen for each class met, came to an agreement, and announced the result to the Council.

The men who planned the United States representative system of government were familiar with the organization of the League of the Iroquois; some say that they developed their ideas from it.

Carved wooden mask
of the Iroquois False Face Society

Wampum

The use of wampum is ancient. The oldest beads were made from a spiral fresh-water shell known to the Iroquois as *otekoa*. This remained their name for wampum when it was later made from other shells. The word we use came from the Algonquian *wampumpeag,* literally "white strings." The white strings were not as important to other Indians as they were to the Iroquois, who wove the beads into belts and strung them on leather thongs. Both strings and belts had meanings "talked" into them. So instructed, they recorded laws and ceremonials and certain events. To a limited extent they also served as messages; no treaty or agreement was binding unless it was

Otekoa,

*the white wampum
strings that were
used as money*

color except for a purple spot slightly bigger than a nickel. Hence there were many white beads and few purple ones. It was by the arrangement of the two colors that the Iroquois made their records.

Quahog wampum beads are cylindrical; an eighth of an inch in diameter and a quarter to a half an inch long. Cutting them from the shell, rounding, polishing, and drilling them with primi-

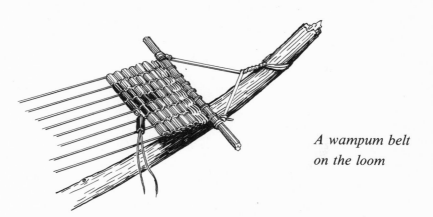

*A wampum belt
on the loom*

tive tools was an appallingly laborious job, compared to which weaving them into belts was easy. When they were woven, the beads formed an integral part of the fabric. The warp ran between the ends of the beads, and two weft threads passed through each bead and enclosed the warp. There's a drawing of part of a wampum belt (they were three feet long) on page 22.

War

Each of the Iroquois nations had its own council, a legislature to run local affairs. These councils could declare war involving their own nations only, though warriors from any other nation were welcome to get into the scrap. Even when the League Council declared war its concern with the matter stopped at that; no troops were mustered, no strategy planned. Anyone who wanted to fight might do so but there was no compulsion.

When war was declared, a hatchet, painted red and decorated with red feathers and black wampum, was struck into the war post in each village. The local war chief (elected) sounded a whoop among the longhouses and started a war dance at the post. The men who joined in the dance were automatically enlisted. Their wives immediately

confirmed by wampum given. A sachem of the Onandaga Nation was the official Keeper of the Wampum and was trained as the interpreter of it.

The beads were always valued by the Indians and always traded, but with one exception they had no fixed value until the white man found them useful as small change and gave them one: a ha'penny per white bead. The Indian exception was the six strings that a murderer must pay the relatives of his victim if they agreed to take cash instead of slaughtering him, as was their right.

Most of the wampum that survives was made from quahog, or hard clam, shells. These may be as much as three inches wide and are white in

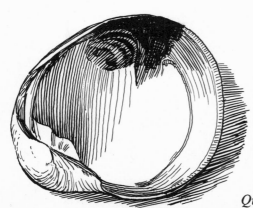

Quahog shell

packed maple sugar and parched corn for rations, and the war party left when the dance was over. Parched corn was boiled first and then dried by slow roasting.

The warriors walked the trail Indian file and they traveled fast. A war party could reach Tennessee from New York in five days. The trails were well established. The principal one, connecting the larger villages of the Five Nations and branching to the smaller ones, ran a crooked course from the Hudson River to Lake Erie. It was a foot and a half wide and was worn six inches into the ground.

On the trail war parties often met and joined forces, but each group remained under its own chief, who wasn't subject to any higher military authority. War tactics, as with all Indians, were chiefly surprise, strike, and run. What was different about the Iroquois was their ferocious savagery. They spared not young or old, women or children. The prisoners they took they never surrendered and they never sought to reclaim their own men who had been captured.

The custom of taking an enemy's scalp must have started as a means of proving at home that you had overcome him. If you had his hair and

A scalp displayed

the skin of his head, there could be little doubt about the matter. White men later collected bounties on scalps they took from Indians. In itself scalping wasn't necessarily fatal, though most people resisted the removal of their hair to the point of death.

The Iroquois brought captured enemies home to be inspected by the community. If a family had lost a man, a captive might be adopted to replace him. He had first to run the gantlet between lines of women and children; if he came through with his head up, he was treated well and became an Iroquois. Captives who were not adopted were tied to a post and turned over to the tender mercies of the women for torture. The stoical endurance of pain was a kind of final grace to the Indian. He schooled himself to it from childhood. Pairs of little boys would rub their foreheads together until one yielded. A warrior, in the course of treatment too dreadful for description, would chat calmly with his captors on matters of topical interest.

War is declared

Weapons

Iroquois bows had their own special shapes. Either the middle was given a reverse curve, like the one illustrated, or the ends were recurved. Ar-

62

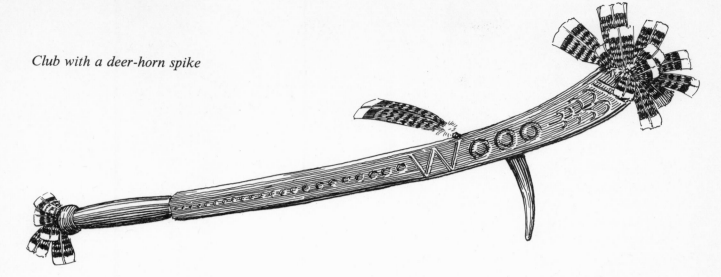

Club with a deer-horn spike

rows were three feet long and feathered spirally. They were sometimes poisoned.

One gets the impression that the Iroquois depended more heavily on war clubs in battle than did other Indians, and the best of their clubs were handsome and deadly implements. There were two kinds of these clubs. One was made of dense, heavy ironwood. It was about two feet long and had a five-inch ball at one end. The war chief in the drawing on page 62 is brandishing one of these. The other was the same length but the ball was replaced by a four-inch spur of deer horn set in the lower edge. Both kinds were usually decorated with patterns and feathers.

The Iroquois had one other weapon which was used by no other North American Indians except the Muskhogee and the Pueblo. It was the blowgun for hunting. These are still used by some South American Indians but most of us don't connect them with "our" Indians. The Iroquois blowgun was a six-foot wooden tube. Its long hole was made by gouging troughs in both halves of a split rod, then reuniting the parts by gluing and lashing. The blowgun dart was made of very light wood. It was about eighteen inches long and not more than an eighth of an inch thick. The head swelled slightly and was usually sharpened. A bunch of hair or other fluff at the other end of the dart served as fletching and also as a piston. A big lungful of air would drive the dart a respectable distance, with enough force to kill small animals and birds.

Clothes

The Iroquois were fundamentally farmers, but at some forgotten time they moved into the woods and began to live as hunters, too. They took over the clothes of the Algonquians because they were well-suited to life in the forests but they adapted them. They either revised details to suit their own ideas or they retained vestiges of a former way of dressing.

Though they sometimes wore breechclouts, for any dressed-up event the men wore deerskin kilts. No other Eastern Indians wore these, except perhaps the Cherokee and the Tuscarora, who were Iroquoian. All Iroquois moccasins were of the

A dart and one end of a blowgun

Iroquois bow and arrow. The hole for the bowstring is unusual.

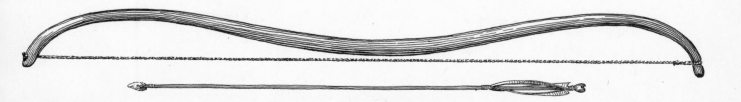

one-piece kind and didn't differ more from Algonquian moccasins than the Algonquian ones differed among those tribes. Leggings were a different matter. Iroquois leggings had no fringe whatever, and instead of being fastened down the side they were seamed up the front, with the seam covered with embroidery or quillwork. These leggings were almost as loose as modern trousers, and they were notched at the bottom, front and back, so they covered the sides of the moccasins and dragged on the ground a little.

In cool weather men wore knee-length shirts made of the usual two hides sewn on the shoulders and up the sides. The side seams were fringed and the fringe was usually carried all the way over the shoulders. The bottom of the shirt also had a deep fringe. These shirts were often ornamented with simple designs made with quills or with sinew or hair embroidery.

The pouch in which an Iroquois man carried his pipe and tobacco was slung from a diagonal shoulder belt. It has been suspected that the belt was copied from the bandolier that a 17th-century white man used for carrying powder charges for his arquebus, but no one seems to have re-

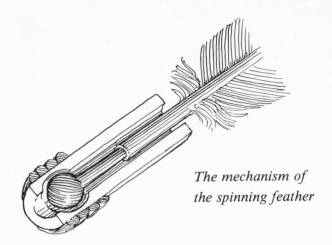

*The mechanism of
the spinning feather*

corded a time when these Indians didn't wear such a belt.

So, too, with the unique feather-covered cap of the Iroquois. Some have said it was recent but nobody can show when it wasn't worn. It was a skull cap, made on a frame and covered entirely with rows of overlapping small feathers. Standing erect on its crown was a short tube of bone with a spherical cavity in its base that retained the ball-shaped end of a wooden pin. When the point of the pin, held upright by the tube, was inserted into the quill of a feather, the gadget held the feather and at the same time allowed it to rotate freely on its axis. The spinning feather gave much the same gay effect as the propeller-topped caps that are now old hat to American boys.

On state occasions important men wore feather bonnets, sometimes two stories high; but there were Algonquians who wore these, too. The bonnets were usually made of wild-turkey feathers and they entirely encircled the head, like a crown.

Women's clothes were basically Algonquian: short leggings and a rather long deerskin skirt. In summer they wore nothing above the waist, but in winter they added a short circular cape, fringed on its lower edge. The cape was slit in two places in front to allow the arms freedom of action.

Iroquois women wore their hair long in a single braid down the back or merely caught into a hank behind, like a pony tail, though not wrapped so near the head. Sachems and shamans, who didn't have to fight, also wore long hair but it wasn't braided or tied; it simply hung loose. Some men wore the Algonquian roach, but more often warriors shaved their heads entirely or wore tufts on the crowns of their heads.

*Iroquois
man and woman*

64

Iroquois longhouse

The Village and the Longhouse

The Iroquois hunted but they weren't primarily hunters. Though in the woods, they remained an agricultural people who lived in more or less permanent villages. They ate more grain and vegetables, not only than other Indians but also more than the early white settlers.

The villages were compact and stockaded in early days, the stakes of the fences inclining outward over dry ditches. The fields needed to supply a sizeable village were several hundred acres in extent and subdivided into family plots by banks of earth. In the plots corn, squash, and beans were planted together in the same hills. Since no fertilizer was used, the land became sterile in about ten years. By that time, too, the local supply of firewood was exhausted and the bark houses were rotten and buggy. So the village was moved; and the bones of the dead went along with the population.

Inside the stockade each clan occupied its longhouse, or longhouses. There was a tendency to increase the length of the house as needed to accommodate the group. Some were 150 feet long but most of them were rather less than half of that. Since there were no openings in the walls except the doors at each end of the house, the middle of a very long one was an inconvenient spot to live.

The framework of one of these structures was of poles, some stout enough to be almost logs. Those on the sides were set vertically four feet

65

apart; they were about ten feet high. Two rows of taller roof supports, each about six feet from the side walls, ran through the inside of the house. The roof was supported on rafters that were bent, but not to a semicircle like those of the wigwam. Each pair of them made a flat pointed arch. The rafters were joined by long purlins, lashed on. The whole surface of the house, walls and roof, was covered with large slabs of elm bark. Poles were tied on over the bark to hold it in place.

At each end of a longhouse there were porches that could be enclosed as temporary vestibules in winter. Directly behind them were permanent vestibules that were used for storage. The rest of the space, on both sides of the twenty-foot width

Inside the longhouse

of the house, was divided by bark partitions into family bunks and storage cells. An ordinary family had one bunk thirteen feet long and six feet wide and one cell six feet by six. The bunk was a shelf a foot high, covered with skins.

Five feet above the bunk was a second shelf the same size. This was used for storage and as a bed for an extra child or two. Food, firewood, clothing, tools, and weapons were all stored together. Ears of dried corn, braided together by their husks, hung from the ceiling and from the roof supports. The front of a bunk was completely open and faced that of the neighbors across the wide aisle. Down the middle of the aisle ran a line of fires, each serving a pair of families. The smoke of these escaped, after a while, through holes in the roof. The whole house was always densely smoky at head height and the inhabitants sat or lay down as much as possible to keep out of it. At those times when fish was being smoked a longhouse was almost unendurable to a white man.

Dogs

Dogs lived in the house and made free of the place. They were of the southern type, short-haired and fairly large, though smaller than a wolf. They were more slender than most modern dogs and had very pointed noses and large pointed ears that stood straight up. Their tails drooped. Iroquois dogs were black, brown, white, or spotted.

Canoes

Perhaps the Iroquois took the idea of building bark canoes from their neighbors, but they never learned to build them very well. They didn't use birch. Most of their boats were made of elm bark, though they also used sycamore and butternut hickory. Enough elm bark for a canoe had to be stripped off a big tree in one piece. It was not reversed as birch bark was; it was too thick for that. The rough outside was scraped to smooth it somewhat.

The resulting canoes were ugly and heavy and they didn't last very long. Whenever an Iroquois had a chance to get hold of an Algonquian birch-bark canoe by barter, theft, or capture, he took advantage of it.

Crafts

These people were quite good woodworkers and their carved bowls, dippers, and cradleboards were neatly made. The grotesque masks they made for the use of their False Face Societies were beautifully executed and almost always deliberately amusing rather than fear-inspiring. These masks were carved on the living tree and removed after the work was complete; otherwise, the carver felt the mask would have no life in it. An apology was made to the tree for this treatment.

Iroquois elm-bark canoe

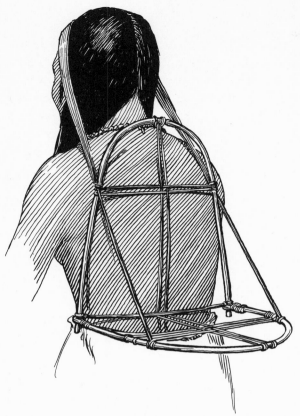

Burden carrier

mented with a few scratched lines, though some pipe bowls had faces or animals modeled on them, always facing the smoker.

Indian tobacco wasn't all of the same variety, but none of it was good. White men couldn't smoke it; neither could the Indians unless they mixed something with it to calm it down. What they mixed in was willow bark, red-osier dogwood bark, or sumac leaves. The Algonquian name for the end product was *kinickinick*. Modern tobacco is the descendant of seeds originally imported from South America.

The Iroquois made pottery because they never found a good substitute until they got the white man's kettles. Iroquois clay pots were round-bottomed. In order to stand one upright a small depression had to be dug for it in the ground; or it could be set in a ring made of twisted grass or brush. The rims of these pots were more often square than round and were decorated with hatchings scratched into the wet clay with a sharp stick or a bone. Similar pots were made by the Mound Builders.

An article that seems to have been used only by the Iroquois was a burden frame they made of hickory withes and basswood fiber. It rested on the carrier's back like a cradleboard and had a kind of shelf at the bottom to support the freight. In addition to the usual tumpline, there was often a chest strap.

Iroquois baskets were made of wooden splints obtained by beating a water-soaked log with a club until the wood fibers loosened and could be stripped off. Some of the baskets were woven, some were plaited, and all were quite coarse in texture.

Pipes and Tobacco

The pottery pipes made by the Iroquois were apparently unique in their time. They were smaller than most Indian pipes and were for casual smoking, with no ceremonial significance. They were shaped with the fingers. Bowl and stem were made as one piece, the rather short stem being molded around a twig that burned away in the heat of firing. The bowl was usually orna-

Pottery pipe

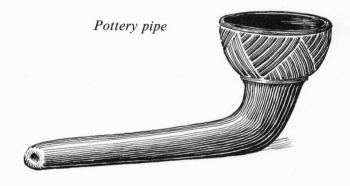

Iroquois clay pot

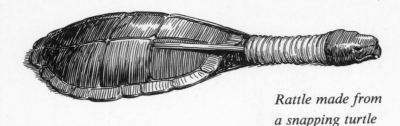

*Rattle made from
a snapping turtle*

Festivals

Six great occasions were celebrated every year, each with several days of ceremonies, feasts, and incidental fun. Their names give an approximation of the dates on which they occurred: the Maple Festival, the Planting, the Strawberry, the Green Corn, the Harvest, and the New Year. The last one, or the first if you prefer, was held nearer to February 1 than to our New Year's Day.

The New Year Festival lasted seven days. All houses were cleaned in preparation for it, and if there was a death in the family, mourning for it was postponed for a week. The first formality was the strangling of a white dog. If a pure-white one couldn't be found, the most nearly white one was used. The dog's body was spotted with red paint and decorated with feathers. Then it was hung from a pole and left there for five days.

On the second day officials visited every house and stirred the fires with special wooden blades. This may have been a vestige of an earlier ceremony in which all fires were extinguished and relighted with a brand from a newly made sacred fire.

During the succeeding days meetings of the False Face Societies were held and there were minor feasts and dances. At one point the boys of the village went masked to each house demanding presents on a trick-or-treat basis. An old woman went with them carrying a basket to collect the gifts. If none were given, the boys were allowed

to return and steal whatever they could. If caught, they had to return the loot at once; if not, it was unclaimable, except by payment when all of the stolen goods were exhibited.

Dream guessing was another feature of the festival, and it was no idle pastime. People recounted their dreams in house after house, and when they were satisfied that they had received a correct interpretation, they would fulfill its demands exactly, regardless of cost, time, or pain, and even if it were suicidal.

At intervals they played games of all sorts. Snowsnake, which the Iroquois had borrowed; lacrosse, which they probably brought with them and may have taught to their neighbors. The Iroquois players used a single lacrosse stick, which looked much like that used in the modern game. In fact the shape and the net of the modern stick were copied from it, though the very ancient Iroquois stick is said to have had no net. The idea of playing the game with a small team, instead of with half the tribe, also originated with the Iroquois.

On the fifth day of the festival the body of the white dog was placed in the Council House. There was chanting and drum beating, and speeches were made over the corpse. White wampum was hung around its neck as a pledge of faith. Then it was carried on a bark litter in procession to the center of the village, and to the accompaniment of more songs and speeches it was cremated. Tobacco leaves were thrown on the fire. The sacrifice did not represent an attempt to load the community's sins upon a scapegoat; it merely dispatched a messenger to the gods to assure them of the continued regard of the people.

After this climax, dances were performed. For the war dance the beat of drums, partly filled with water, accented war songs whose words were in an ancient lost language that no one understood. As in all war dances, the step was a stomp; it was

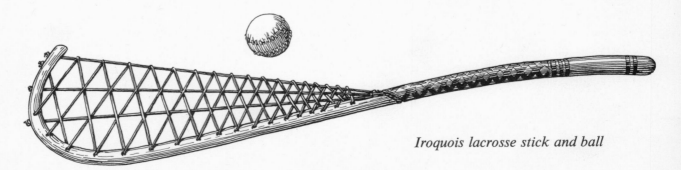

Iroquois lacrosse stick and ball

the menacing gestures of the performers that gave variety. The war whoop and a resounding chorus response began the performance. Lewis H. Morgan described the Iroquois version of the war whoop as a prolonged yell on a high note that slid downward and then ended with a short yell on the original note. Thus:

Ah a a a a a a a   Ahm!
            a
               a
                  a

A group of twenty or so performed the ancient feather dance, as mild as the war dance was violent. It too, however, was a stomp dance done in full dress to a fast beat marked by two singers with turtle-shell rattles. Full dress meant: feathered cap; kilt and shoulder belt; short leggings and moccasins; plus arm bands, wristbands, and deer-hoof knee rattles. A light war club and a scalping knife were carried.

After the dances a feast was held in the Iroquois manner: everyone brought his dish to the public cooking place, had it filled, and then took the food home and ate it in peace.

The two days of festival that were still left were given over to celebration and to playing the plum-stone game, which required at least that long to finish. It was played in the Council House by teams of considerable size. Individuals played in pairs and in turn. The game, which completely enraptured the whole group, was nothing more than an elaboration of heads-or-tails played with six wild-plum stones which had been smoothed up and painted dark on one side, light on the other. The stones were shaken together in a wooden bowl and dumped, in the hope that all six would show the same color. Five had to show alike to count at all; anything less lost the player the right to make the next throw. There was an elaborate system of counting and a bank. The game went on until one side had won everything. It had an obscure religious significance.

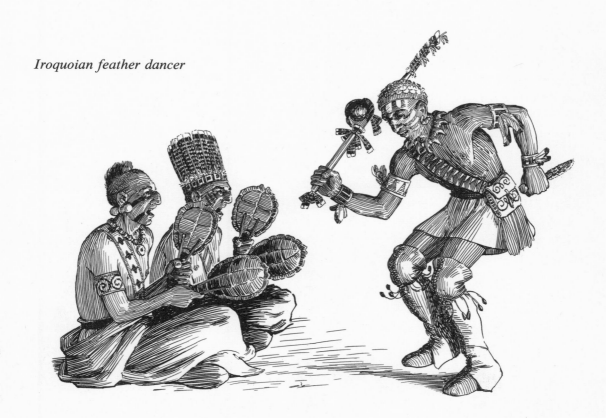

Iroquoian feather dancer

*Muskhogean village
(reconstructed)*

5

The Southern Farmers

Under many tribal names the Muskhogeans occupied the whole Southeast from the Mississippi to the Atlantic and from the Appalachian foothills to the Gulf. They came from the north and west. They had some remote connection with the Mexican Indians and a much less remote one with the temple-mound builders. They displaced an earlier and quite different people, remnants of whom were pushed far down the Florida peninsula. Later the whites displaced the Muskhogeans and some of them, with other refugees, retreated into Florida. They absorbed the tribes there and are now called Seminoles. The name is said to have come from the Spanish *cimarrón*, meaning wild.

The Southeastern Indians came into contact with Europeans so early and were so quickly changed that much we would like to know about them is lost. The principal tribe was the Muskhogee, called Creeks by the English. They were pretty well spread across the territory and were the dominant force in the loose organization of tribes speaking related languages that was known as the Creek Confederacy. There were other Muskhogean tribes, like the Chickasaw and the Choctaw, that didn't belong to the Confederacy.

Towns

Muskhogean towns seem to have been located and built with some idea of real permanence. There was a plaza and each clan had its own section. Some towns had fairly straight streets and blocks of residences, each with its private garden plot. The land, however, was "owned" only during occupancy and was not purchased. The plaza wasn't entirely open ground; at one end there was an artificial mound with ceremonial buildings on it. In some towns the chief's house was also on the mound. The rest of the plaza was taken up by the chungke yard, a rectangular space for games, dances, and other amusements.

The residence of a prosperous Muskhogee had four separate buildings facing an open court. One was the winter lodge, small and warm, which served in all seasons as a kitchen. Another was the summer house and reception hall. It was quite open and as airy as possible. A third building was used for the storage of provisions. One end of this was enclosed; the other was an open shed where tools and gear were kept. Some of these provision houses were said by William Bartram to have had two stories, with a private council room on the second floor and a porch over the shed. This has a suspiciously European ring to it. The fourth building was also a storehouse; in it were kept hides or other goods for trading. The buildings in the illustrations are reconstructions based on descriptions and on old drawings of the houses of related Indians. There is a possibility that all Muskhogee houses were once round.

Outside the town, and perhaps surrounding it, were the fields that provided the main source of food. They were divided into family plots by low banks of earth but they were worked cooperatively by all the men and women together under overseers. In addition to the usual corn and squash, these people raised sweet potatoes and melons. Men marched to the fields in procession carrying hoes with blades of stone or of the shoulder blades of animals. The women followed, carrying food. As they worked the fields they sang in unison. There was a fine for shirking work.

Children guarded newly planted seed from the crows all day. Later in the season, the men guarded the fields at night to keep raccoons and woodchucks from the ripening corn. Each family had its own corncrib and each family contributed to the Miko's crib, which was a reserve supply for emergency and for public uses, such as supplying war parties, feeding visitors, and helping out other towns that had lost their crops.

Clan Organization

The Muskhogeans had a clan system similar to that of the Iroquois, but there were many more clans, at least fifty. Though there was a division of the clans into a "White" group and a "Red" group, it placed no restrictions on marriage. Individuals were prohibited, however, from marrying within their own clan, and marriage between certain clans was tabooed because traditional connections made them relatives.

The White clans held a superior position. It was their leaders who selected the chief, or Miko, who was always a member of the same "royal" clan. The Miko had much more power than Indian chiefs usually had; and he was given more personal homage than Indian chiefs generally received. He was surrounded by attendants and on state occasions he was carried on a litter.

For official appearances the Miko wore a swan-feather bonnet and painted half of his face red and the other half black. When he was dressed informally he merely painted a red circle around one eye and a black one around the other. Face painting was formalized among these people so that certain colors and patterns showed a man's status and also what town he came from. Old drawings suggest that the Creeks once went in for elaborate tattooing.

Priests, healers, wizards, and storytellers got special training and took a series of degrees, each higher one requiring a longer period of fasting. A "Ph.D." who had completed a twelve-day fast was entitled to paint red lines outward from the corners of his mouth.

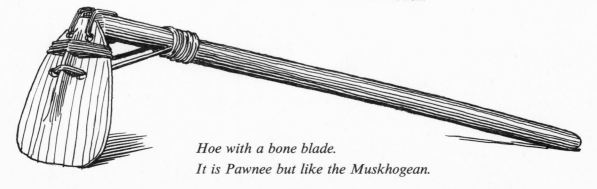

Hoe with a bone blade.
It is Pawnee but like the Muskhogean.

The Miko

Justice

As elsewhere, justice was on an eye-for-an-eye basis, perhaps judged by the Miko, but executed by the family of the injured party. It was carried to such lengths that even the accidental injuries of children were equalized. Murder could sometimes be paid off, not with wampum but with large white beads, known as hair tubes, that were made from the central columns of conch shells.

Infanticide was commonplace. Twins were abhorred; no one raised an eyebrow if the mother killed one or both of them. In fact, a mother might and often did kill her child during the first month of its life. The very old and the hopelessly sick were killed as an act of mercy, but never with the idea of getting rid of them.

Marriage

Weddings were originally arranged by the women of the clans, both principals being left in complete ignorance until they were brought together for the ceremony. Even in later days when a young man picked his girl and bought her, her father's opinion in the matter wasn't asked.

The contract of marriage was sealed by the bridegroom breaking an ear of corn and giving half of it to his bride, along with a symbolical deer's foot. They were not legally married, however, until the man had left a deer carcase at his bride's door and she had carried it into the house, cooked it, and fed him some of it before witnesses.

Though no restrictions of continence were placed on anyone before marriage, the faithfulness of husband and wife was expected to be complete and any laxity was punished by mutilation. If a man's wife died, he might not remarry for four months. A widow had to remain single for four years, unless she married her late husband's brother. The brother, regardless of the fact that he already had a wife, was under an obligation to marry the widow. A family also felt obliged to provide a new wife for a son-in-law who had lost one.

Children

Newborn babies were bathed in cold water; and this was but the first of many cold baths. Every Muskhogee plunged into the water four times upon arising, summer and winter.

A mother had complete charge of her children, although her brothers took an interest in the training of the boys. Children were well treated and were shown great affection but they were punished when they misbehaved. Punishment was by scratching the legs with a sharp awl deeply enough to draw blood. This was thought to let out the evil that had caused the mischief and also to lessen the child's fear of losing blood.

Boys slept on panther skins, girls on fawn skins, so that each would absorb the qualities of the animals. A girl was named for life; but a boy kept his name only until he could earn a better one by prowess. With each advance he made in the tribal scale he received an entirely new name which, by the way, he would not speak himself. When a boy's voice changed he went off by himself to fast for days. This practice inured the strong to hardship and killed off the weak.

A boy was considered to be born with a kind of original sin; he was in disgrace until he had proved himself. No matter what his talents or merits, he did menial work and had no standing in the community until he had brought in a scalp. Scalps

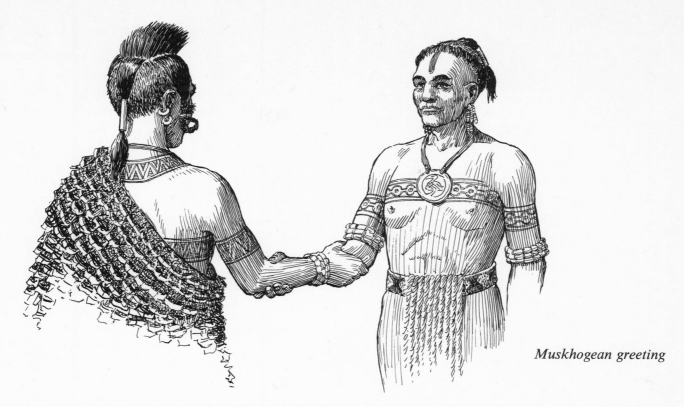

Muskhogean greeting

weren't easily come by and they were of such importance that a single one was often divided to give several a share in the glory. So essential was a young man's first scalp that he would sometimes murder a friend to get it.

Manners and Customs

When Indians met they didn't shake hands. The Northeasterner rubbed his own chest and then that of his friend. The Muskhogeans came a little nearer to modern convention; they grasped one another's arms. When two men wished to pledge friendship they scratched each other with the toothed jawbone of a gar fish. In the later days of rum, drinkers came out of a bout scratched all over. This ritual scratching got into nearly everything. Players were scratched before a lacrosse game; warriors were scratched when they were promoted.

There was a special whoop exchanged between friends. All Muskhogean whoops were classified; there were different ones to proclaim news, defiance, death, and the taking of a scalp. In addition, the Muskhogeans had a highly developed sign language, now lost, that is said to have depended more on pantomime than on prearranged signals, as in the western Plains.

A private family would readily take in an outlander clansman, but strangers were more often entertained publicly by the town. They were fed from the Miko's crib and they slept in the Hot House, the men's club, or in a special guest house. One finds no record of the entertainment of traveling women, only men.

The usual courteous silence was maintained at the outset of a visit, but it was short. There was always much informal chatting and long-winded speechifying. A returning traveler entertained the company in the Hot House for hours with a minutely detailed and completely truthful account of his experiences.

The Muskhogeans avoided hurting anyone's feelings, but another's mishap, even a serious accident, would send them into ground-rolling spasms of mirth. Most Indians maintained a free-and-easy, kidding relationship with their brothers-in-law; a Muskhogee extended it to all members of his own clan and to all men whose fathers were members of his father's clan. Though the Creeks paid little attention to it, other Muskhogean tribes required that a man avoid his mother-in-law and a woman her father-in-law. Direct speech or physical contact between them was expected to make both itch all over, and since it was expected, it probably did.

If a man died on a journey, his body was left on a scaffold until it disintegrated; then his bones were brought to his family. If he died at home, he was buried sitting up, along with all of his personal

possessions, in a round hole under the bed in his house. His body was left barefoot so the living wouldn't hear his ghost walking. The ghost was believed to stay on the premises for four days. During that time a bright fire burned in the lodge and the widow lay mourning on the grave. All Indians could be pretty gruesome about the dead. These Southerners cleaned the bones of important people and stored them in special buildings under guard.

Trade

Long before they ever heard of a white man the Southeastern Indians engaged in real business. The inland tribes had mica, copper, pipestone, and flint; the coast tribes had salt, sea shells, dried fish, and the evergreen yaupon, whose leaves were used for an essential ceremonial drink. These things they exchanged and from the earliest times they used conch-shell hair tubes as money. One tube was worth four deerskins in the interior.

Though they couldn't write, they could count by scratching marks on the ground with a stick. They used a decimal system. The unit was one vertical mark, and a plus mark stood for ten,

though it was probably only a tally and was not itself counted.

Short lengths were measured by parts of the body; a knuckle length, a hand span, an arm stretch, and so on. Long distances were roughly estimated by traveling time: so many "sleeps" between here and there. They couldn't date past events very far back and not within closer limits than a month. They did better with the near future. When an assembly was called to meet in seven days, a man expecting to attend made up a bundle of seven sticks. One was thrown away every day; when there were none left, it was time to go.

Travel and Boats

There were marked trails everywhere. Rafts that all might use were moored at river crossings, though it was sometimes necessary to swim the river in order to reach the raft. The many streams were themselves trails for dugouts. The coastal Indians even went to sea in these craft, fishing from them, trading along the shore, and sometimes voyaging as far as Cuba.

Indians in general used dugouts far more than canoes. Dugouts were made even in birch-bark country; but the Southerners had no other kind of boat. In the middle-Atlantic area the tulip poplar was the canoe tree and was so named. It

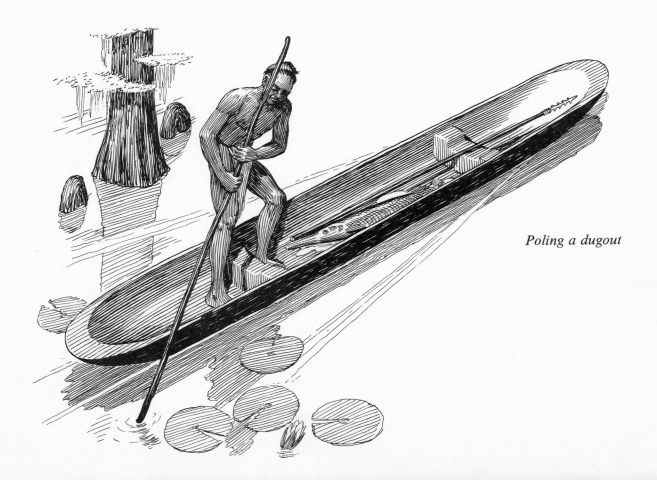

Poling a dugout

grows very tall and straight in the woods and de-
velops a thick trunk that tapers but little. Until a
few years ago there was still a very tall one in
Maryland with a butt a full ten feet in diameter.
Tulip wood is heavy when it's green but it be-
comes light when it dries. It's soft and easily
worked, and though it isn't resistant to rot, it holds
up quite well with careful treatment.

South of the James River most dugouts were
made of cypress, which also attains impressive
size, or did when it had a chance. Perhaps because it grows with its feet in the water, sound
cypress is impervious to damage by moisture. It
is also light and strong. The Indians didn't bother
to cut down a cypress for a boat; they used fallen
trees. The wood is durable, but dead trees topple
in time, and they were perhaps better for the purpose than green ones.

Much of the work of hollowing out and shaping
a log for a dugout was done with fire; only the
finishing was done with stone tools: axes, gouges,
and chisels. Shells were used for scrapers. The
outside of the boat was finished first. This was
chiefly a matter of shaping the identical ends,
though some wood was taken off the bottom to
flatten it and quite a lot was split off the top of
the log before excavation began. When the shape
was satisfactory, holes were bored here and there
in the bottom to the depth of its finished thickness, an inch and a half.

Pine pitch was soaked into the wood to hasten
the action of the fires that burned out the inside.
Fanning the fire also speeded things up. It must
have been necessary to watch the burning very
carefully because fire can eat deeply into wood
without giving outside notice of its progress.
Probably sections were doused and inspected and
then refired if they needed it. When the fire exposed the ends of the holes drilled in the bottom of
the log, burning had gone deep enough and the
inside was cleaned up by chipping and scraping.
The holes were plugged.

The sides of a dugout were about half an inch
thick at the gunwale, becoming gradually thicker
toward the bottom. Some dugouts were completely excavated, like troughs, but more often two
bulkheads of the wood were left to strengthen the
hull. Most Indian dugouts were round-ended, had
no sheer whatever, and no rise at bow or stern, but
some—notably those of the Natchez on the
Mississippi and those of the unrelated Menomini
west of Lake Michigan—were shaped in what appears to be an imitation of a birch-bark canoe.

The surfaces of log boats, especially those made
of tulip wood, were greased frequently with animal
fat, which preserved the wood and kept it from
becoming water-logged. Probably the fat was put
on hot so it would penetrate. Dugouts could be
paddled, or poled if the water was shallow enough.
Drawings made in the 16th century by John

White show Indians fishing from dugouts that have fires burning in them for warmth, presumably burning on sand.

Clothing

A Southern warrior seldom wore a breechclout; he simply hung a fringe of shredded mulberry bark from his belt, which was often made of snakeskin. He almost always wore garters on his leggings, though he was less likely to wear leggings than an Algonquian. His robe for dressy occasions was often covered with bird feathers, with their quills caught in a twined weave of mulberry bark. Moccasins were for ceremonies and for travel; everybody went barefoot around home.

A warrior wore a pouch slung from one shoulder. In it were his pipe and tobacco and a small leather packet containing a quartz crystal, known as a *sobia,* and some powered red paint. To the sobia was attributed such a power of magic that its owner wouldn't think of touching it, or even looking at it uncovered.

A Muskhogean's hair was sometimes cut in a roach, but it was on the front of his head, with a braided "lovelock" on either side and a scalp lock, pulled through a hair tube, hanging behind. From the crown back, the hair was either cut very short or the head was plucked bare. Some men preferred a circular tonsure, like a monk's. Everybody soaked his hair in bear grease. At festivals men who rated them wore swan-feather bonnets and hung engraved shell disks, called gorgets, around their necks.

A short skirt of deerskin or of Spanish moss and a necklace or two sufficed as summer clothing for the women. In winter they added a tunic of twined-weave mulberry bark, hung over one shoulder. Women wore their hair long, loose, and greasy. In a few tribes it was bound up in back after marriage.

Weapons and Hunting

The Muskhogee carried a quiver and bow case made of panther skin with the fur left on, and he had a fine bow of hickory or black locust to put into it. Most of his arrows were cane, which grows perfectly straight but is light and rather brittle; so cane arrows had wooden foreshafts to support the points and to give weight to the front ends so that they would fly straight.

Blowguns were used all over the South for killing birds and small animals. A few of the Southern Indians used slings for the same kind of game. This is remarkable because few other Indians ever used slings. A cane knife was another almost exclusively Southern article. It was simply a short length of stout cane with one end cut on a long slant and probably hardened with fire. It seems incredible that this would cut anything tougher than soup, but apparently it would.

The ceremonial preparation for a hunt and the superstitious taboos connected with hunting make it seem hardly worth the trouble. The hunter took a preliminary sweat bath, sitting in a little hut and singing and praying as he poured water over hot stones that were supplied to him from the outside. He cooled off with a plunge in the creek. Almost all Indians took sweat baths on slight provocation. Then he drank magic medicine and applied it to his weapons. On the trail, he burned tobacco leaves in all his campfires to ward off malevolent spirits, and just to be safe he paid a shaman one deerskin to go along and work magic on the spot as needed. If the hunter tired, he scratched his own thigh and bled a little to increase his strength.

Large hunting parties often took deer by surrounding a herd and driving them into prepared pockets. Fire sometimes helped in the driving. A lone hunter depended on stalking. He disguised himself with a whole deerskin and approached stealthily, making sure the wind was blowing from the game toward him. Bears were hunted chiefly for the thick layer of fat under their skins. Buffalo weren't unknown game in the Southeast long ago; their big shoulder blades were valued as hoes.

A hunter always gave some of his meat to his parents and allotted some to the town's widows and orphans. A fisherman did the same with the catch he hooked, speared, trapped, poisoned, or shot with arrows.

War

Curiously, it wasn't the mighty hunters among the Indians who were the militarists; it was the well-fed farmers, who had leisure to devote to

Cane knife
about nine inches long

Deerstalking

war. The exceptions were the Plains Indians, who made an easy living on buffalo; the Navaho and the Apache of the Southwest, hunters who made much of their living by pillage; and the Northwesterners, who lived easy on fish; and, in another way, the Pueblos, who were farmers but just naturally didn't care for fighting.

Nowhere was the war game played with more enthusiasm than in the Southeast. And it was a game; it wasn't real war. No tribe wanted to conquer another tribe or exterminate it. They just wanted excitement and scalps; when they had those, the war was over, except that the losers were certain to start it up again. It's recorded that the Muskhogeans went forth to war with shields and with rawhide helmets and breastplates, but no one remembers what they looked like.

All the members of a war party fasted for three days and then imbibed the usual magic drink before setting out. They wouldn't rest on the trail in daylight. Thirty or forty warriors might start, but anyone who had the wrong dream or heard the wrong bird singing would immediately go home with the full approval of his mates.

The war chief had won the right to his position and held it only so long as his luck was good. He or his specially consecrated lieutenant carried the Sacred Ark—a name devised by a white man

with the lost tribes of Israel on his mind. The Ark must have been a nuisance because it was twenty inches long with ends a foot square. It was supposed to contain the horns of a mythical snake and the bones of a mythical panther. These were of such potent power that no one except the two responsible men would touch the Ark. As the enemy shared this fear, the burden could be useful.

Very long ago the Muskhogeans tortured only those prisoners whom they deemed guilty of some outrage; the others they adopted. But torture is habit-forming. In later days they continued to adopt young men, but all middle-aged captives were "devoted to death." The head of the prisoner was covered with clay to protect his precious scalp. Tethered by a grapevine to a slave post in the chungke yard, he shouted his war songs while the women slowly scorched him to death with torches of dry grass.

After this and some extremely unattractive dissection, the Beloved Men—shamans, who wore white circles on their foreheads and were forbidden to kill—awarded new names to the successful warriors. The candidates presented themselves greased all over with bear oil, wearing red moccasins, an otter skin on each leg, and a collar of swan feathers. Their faces were painted in vertical streaks. They were duly scratched and as they were rechristened fifteen-inch-high crowns of white swan feathers were placed on their heads.

The Square

The central square of each town was divided into two parts: the Mound, with the Hot House and the Cabin Court on it, and the chungke yard at ground level.

The Hot House was both a winter temple and a men's club. It was a circular building fifty feet in diameter with walls of vertical posts plastered with mud. Bartram mentions that the outside wall was painted with bizarre murals, but he didn't copy them. The conical roof was bark or thatch, with no smoke hole whatever in its top. So large a roof had to be supported by two additional rings of posts on the inside of the house. The narrow entrance was protected by a ten-foot overlap of the walls.

Inside, a fire burned in the center of the room. Its dry barkless wood, used to keep down smoke, was arranged in a spiral so that it burned continuously without attention. Encircling it around the sides of the room were two wide benches, or beds, built like steps and covered with mats and skins. Here each accredited warrior had his place where he might loaf and smoke and chat with his peers, or simply sleep. Music and dancing (male) were sometimes provided. No women ever entered the Hot House, and in view of its probable stench, they were lucky.

The Hot House was unbearable in summer, so the gentlemen moved to the Cabin Court. Here there were more tiered benches, but they were ranged in four separate cabins which formed the sides of a square. The cabins were open at the eaves in back and fully at front and ends, and were oriented to the Four Winds. The cabins were forty feet long and places in them were allotted to clans. One, the Beloved Cabin, was sacred. Behind its benches, a long narrow room was considered the holy of holies; it was never unguarded by a Beloved Man.

A hero gets a new name

The White, or central, seat in the Beloved Cabin was reserved for the Miko. Here he and honored guests sat fanning themselves with eagle tails, lighting their pipes from fire pots that stood on the elbow-high partitions between the benches, and solacing themselves with cooling drinks while dancers performed before them. Here, too, the Miko presided over the Council and meted out justice. Before his seat, honors were awarded to heroes.

Chungke

The third feature of the square, the chungke yard, was a rectangular space made level with sand and surrounded on three sides by banked earth. It was the playing field for the ancient game of chungke but it had other uses. In its center a tall pole topped with an animal skull was the target for an informal ball game played by the women against the men. In the two corners farthest from the mound stood the slave posts, club-shaped and capped with human skulls, where captives were tethered for torture. Ceremonies and dances involving the whole population were held in the chungke yard.

The game of chungke was at least as old as the burial-mound builders and probably much older. Variations of it were played all over America. The classic game was played by two men, each with an eight-foot pole tapered to flat points at its ends. The players used one chungke stone between them. It belonged to the town. A disk, concave on both sides and with a convex edge, it was an inch and a half thick and five inches or less across.

The two players ran abreast down the field and one bowled the stone on edge ahead of them. Still

Chungke stone

79

running, each man threw his pole as he would a javelin. The object was not to hit the stone but rather to have the pole land where the stone stopped rolling. It took practice and nice judgment. The nearer pole scored one point; a pole actually touching the stone counted two. Indians would run up and down the field all day playing this game and bet their whole wardrobes on it.

The Busk

This was the Green Corn Feast, held in midsummer, that started the year anew for the Muskhogeans. The word *Busk* is the white man's corruption of the Creek word *poskita*. It was an old ceremony and had some connection with the abstract idea of peace, which appealed to the Indians—so long as they didn't have to take it literally—much as it appeals to us.

There was a general purification at the start. Houses and clothing were cleaned and old articles were discarded and replaced. All disputes were settled and all debts were paid. There was a general round of sweat bathing and scratching. All of

the men fasted and then, in order of rank, partook ritually of the Black Drink, which they loved.

This concoction was peculiar to the Southeast. It was brewed from the leaves of the hollylike yaupon (*ilex vomitoria*). The liquor was as black as tar and is said to have tasted like strong tea. It was drunk hot from large gourds. This tea was supposed to shrive; and to promote all virtues. A warrior downed a quart of the stuff, and half an hour later would grasp his abdomen with his forearms and deliberately and forcibly regurgitate it. He was admired if he could spout eight feet.

When everything and everybody was purified, all the fires in town were put out, even the fire in the Hot House. In the Cabin Court the wood for a new fire was laid; four sticks pointing to the Four Winds. Four symbolic ears of green corn were laid across the sticks so that their ends touched and they formed a square. With prayer and incantation, the chief of the Beloved Men spun a stick between his palms to create the new and sacred fire. From it, all the town fires were relighted and the warriors broke fast with the first green corn cooked over them.

Lacrosse

The Busk went on for some time and included other ceremonies and ritual dances as well as social dances and games. The principal game was lacrosse played in what seems to have been its oldest form, each man with two sticks and each team having about sixty men, representing the Whites and the Reds.

The field needed was 500 yards long, far bigger than the chungke yard. The goals were limber poles spaced nine feet apart. The oldest balls are said to have been solid wood, but leather ones stuffed hard with deer hair are the only kind known to have been used. The players were forbidden to touch the ball; they caught it, carried it, and threw it with their sticks. Each player used two identical sticks far smaller than a modern one. They played barefoot, wearing a breechclout and an ornamental tail of some sort. The bodies of one team were painted white, which made a strong contrast between the teams because Muskhogeans were darker than most Indians. Before the game everyone was well scratched, took a sweat bath and a swig of the Black Drink, and danced all night.

At the start of the game both teams lined up facing each other down the length of the field. An

Muskhogean lacrosse

The Natchez "Sun"
(most of the detail
in this illustration
is necessarily conjectural)

old man threw the ball high in the center and ducked. There ensued a ten-minute struggle before anyone was able to get the ball into open play. Arms and legs were accidentally broken in scrimmage, but it was all in good fun and there was seldom any fouling.

Game was twenty points. Score was kept by setting a stake in the ground for each point made by each team until there were ten; then removing them one at a time until the winning side had none. A bowl of "medicine" with a piece of turtle hide in it was set behind each goal to attract the ball, and the playing sticks were anointed with similar stuff. Each team had a medicine ball that could be used for one goal only. It contained a measuring worm believed to make the ball invisible to the other side, in spite of contrary evidence.

A game lasted about an hour and a half. At its end the losers ran for home to avoid the jeers of the winners, who marched around their goal and then held a stomp dance.

Natchez Royalty

The Natchez were Muskhogeans who lived on the Mississippi River. They were not a very large tribe, but their system of social classes was too remarkable to omit. They were obviously temple-mound people originally, for they still had temples on their mounds, with sacred fires in them constantly tended by priests. They worshipped the sun and their king, for he was that, who was known as the Great Sun. He had absolute authority and his person was sacred. His foot was not allowed to touch the earth. He was carried everywhere on a litter, and if it was necessary for him to walk, mats were spread on the ground before him.

When a Great Sun died his wives were strangled—it is said, voluntarily—and buried with him.

82

Alive, it was his function to howl at the rising sun, bowing three times. He then blew smoke to the Four Winds from his sacred pipe. When he had done that he made a lordly gesture to show the sun what path to follow and went in to breakfast.

The Natchez divided themselves into four social classes: Suns, Nobles, Honored People, and alas, Stinkards. The odium of being a Stinkard was relieved somewhat by the fact that the upper classes all had to marry Stinkards. Even the Great Sun himself had a Sun mother and a Stinkard father. All members of the Sun class were in the same situation. It was more complex with the Nobles; they had Sun fathers and Stinkard mothers, or Noble mothers and Stinkard fathers. The same idea applied to the Honored People; they had either Honored mothers or Noble fathers. The children of Honored men were immutably Stinkards.

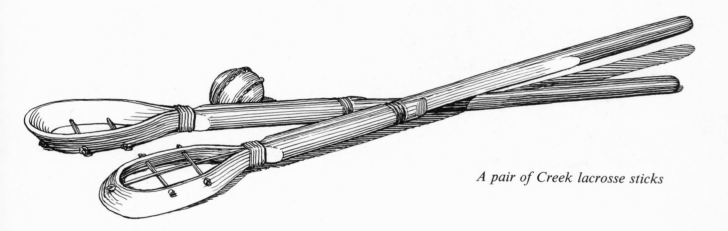

A pair of Creek lacrosse sticks

Mandan earth lodges

6

The Midlands

Up the middle of the continent, below the Great Lakes and mostly west of the Mississippi River, Indians farmed some of the most productive land in the world. They spoke several languages but they all lived pretty much the same kind of lives.

The Caddo had been a farming people in what is now northeastern Texas for more than two thousand years. Many tribes had broken off from them in that time and some had moved northward up the river valleys—the Pawnee to Nebraska, the Arikara to North Dakota, for instance. Other tribes who spoke Siouan dialects had also moved into the midlands; *they* said from the East. This may have been true, for a lot of their ideas were strikingly like those of the Muskhogeans. The Mandan are the best-known of these Siouans, not because they were the most important, but because early white visitors found them approachable and reported upon them. Their towns were far up the Missouri Valley.

Mandan villages were often built on a promontory above a river so as to provide a good view of water-borne visitors and so as to have but one land approach. The towns were usually fortified. The round houses in them differed from those of any Indians that have been discussed here. For one thing they were big—forty to sixty feet in diameter and fifteen feet high; for another, they were strong. They were framed with big posts and beams and covered with turf over thatch. Mandans customarily took the air in the evenings sitting on their dome-shaped roofs; most Indian housetops wouldn't have stood the strain. Each house had a vestibule on its east side, framed of logs. The floor of the house was of earth but the Mandan hardened it by wetting it down and burning bundles of grass on it.

A big lodge was occupied by several related families with their dogs and possessions. Later, they kept the choicest of their mounts inside, too, not for the comfort of the horses, but to keep them from being stolen. The center space under the smoke hole, where there was heat and a little light, was the common living room for the occupants. A little privacy for sleeping and loafing was managed in closely curtained bedsteads that were set near the outer walls. These "four-posters" seem to have been unique to the Mandan. The Mandan made pottery and quite handsome baskets of unusual design.

The Pawnee, whose roots were quite different from the Mandan, built similar earth lodges with very long vestibules that made them the shape of oversize igloos. The floors were dug out a little to leave an earthen bench all the way around the inside of the house. Distant cousins of the Pawnee who farmed further south needed no more shelter than beehive-shaped grass huts gave them. Their ancestral tribe, the Caddo, built cabins with walls of close-set posts and roofs of thatch. Caddo houses were copied by early French settlers in the Mississippi Valley.

Bullboats

All of these Indians lived along rivers, hence they had boats. Since these were used chiefly as ferries, any old kind of boat would do. What they had was, indeed, any old kind of boat! It was called a bullboat and it was clumsier than either the moosehide canoe or the elm-bark one. In shape it was a big bowl. It was made of rawhide stretched over a crude frame of saplings. Two paddlers could coerce it, but one man alone had trouble making it do more than go round and round. It was useful for covering the smoke hole of an earth lodge in wet weather, however.

Mandan "four-poster" bed

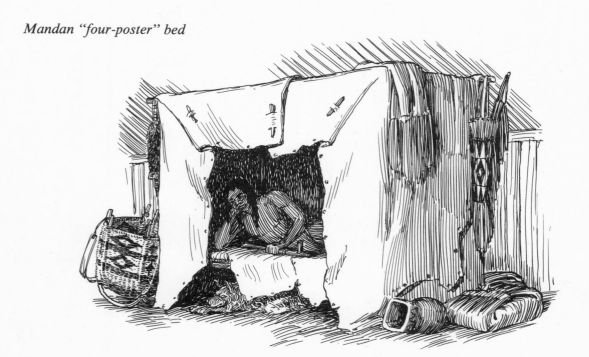

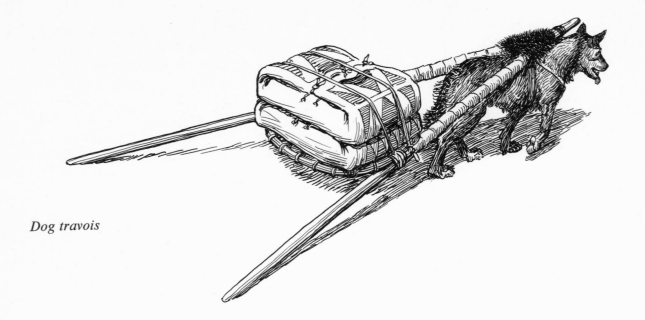

Dog travois

Midland Indians were farmers first, but they all shared another activity; they hunted buffalo. Near their farms the Great Plains, almost empty of humans, stretched to the foothills of the Rocky Mountains. The Plains hadn't enough rainfall for agriculture but their grass supported tens of thousands of grazing animals, of which the buffalo was the largest and probably the most plentiful. The Indians weren't able to follow the herds then, as they did later with horses, but whenever the animals came within range the farmers put aside their hoes and went after them.

A buffalo hunt was a difficult and dangerous expedition. All of the active members of the tribe went along, packing food and shelter with them. These Indians trained their dogs to help with the transport job by carrying packs or by dragging tent poles and small travois on which burdens could be lashed. Their shelters were tepees, but the size of the tepee was limited by the length of the poles the dogs could drag and it was barely big enough to huddle in. The added burdens of meat and green hides made the carrying problem worse on the trip home. The midlanders deliberately crossed their ordinary curs with coyotes to get stronger dogs. The resulting animals could carry up to fifty pounds on their backs.

One way of hunting buffalo was by stalking, which was done by individual hunters. The hunter prepared himself by offering prayers to the buffalo god and by taking a sweat bath to rid himself as far as possible of his human smell. Then he disguised himself with a wolfskin. (Buffalo were impervious to attack by wolves, so they gave him little attention.) The same disguise was used for locating herds and came to be used for scouting in war. Creeping forward in the grass from downwind, and trying to show only as a wolf, the hunter

Buffalo hunt on foot

put himself as near his quarry as possible, despite the risk, for bison had thick hides and he seldom had a chance for a second arrow. He tried to pick an animal grazing a little away from the main herd. Rarely was it a bull; the danger was great enough without adding to it. A lone man on foot had practically no chance at all against a wounded buffalo bull.

More often, however, a whole band went after a whole herd. The ground for such a hunt was carefully prepared and was used for years. A strong corral was made at the foot of a cliff, and on the plain above it two long converging lines of rock piles were built. The piles were fairly close together and behind each one an Indian was hidden. A shaman then presented himself before the buffalo herd and by odd gestures and much magic invited the animals into the trap. Perhaps it was curiosity that brought them within the stone-marked lines, but if the wind was right, they came. Once in, their seducer turned aside and the men behind the outermost cairns rose up shouting and waving blankets. The buffalo stampeded toward the cliff, running ever faster as noise and terror built up behind them. Over they went, falling into the corral, and the rest of the story was slaughter and waste. A cliffless variant on this method was to stampede a herd between two lines of hidden archers, who picked off as many as they could. Either way was death for somebody if the animals turned aside. Herds were also surrounded by grass fires and slaughtered.

Dakota in full feather

7

The Buffalo Hunters

The whole world's mental picture of an American Indian is a Dakota of the Plains draped in beaded buckskin, and panoplied with feathers, bestraddling a piebald mustang. When the first white men landed on the East coast, the Dakotas were in the north woods, living the lives of canoe Indians in bark wigwams, much as their enemies, the Chippewa, lived. They'd never seen a horse; neither had the midland farmers to the south of them.

When the Spanish came into New Mexico in 1598 they brought horses to a land where there were none. Some of their horses escaped to the equine heaven of the Plains. Here they multiplied so phenomenally that in less than a century there were herds of wild horses everywhere. Needing a name for them, the Indians called them "big dogs." No one can say surely how they learned that horses could be broken and ridden. The earliest record of an Indian on horseback is dated 1700 and shows the rider *tied* on his mount. This didn't last long.

Soon these men were magnificent horsemen. Stirrups? No. Saddles were for women; a warrior needed only a folded blanket and a girth. His bridle was a simple halter with one rein and usually no bit whatever in the horse's mouth. Indian horses were accustomed to being mounted from the right-hand side. This gave white men trouble when they tried to ride them; conversely, Indians had trouble when they stole horses from white men. Shortly every Indian had at least one horse, and some had many. Horses were wealth; they yielded a profit from no investment at all. In winter a few cottonwood branches were cut so the animals could nibble on the buds; otherwise they were expected to forage for themselves.

Now the buffalo hunt that had been so arduous became a magnificent sport. A horse could outrun a buffalo and he could be trained to run close alongside one, so that his rider had ample opportunity to place his arrows or wield his spear. The Indians got flintlock guns from white traders early in the 19th century and cut the barrels short to make them handier on horseback, but a flintlock was slow to load and an Indian with a gun always had his bow also. Best of all, with horses one hunt wasn't the end of the thing; when the herd moved, the tribe could move with it.

After horses were acquired, the hunting of buffalo by individuals was frowned upon. A single

Dog Soldier.
The feathered bustle was worn only for dancing.

hunter might get an animal or two, but he might also stampede the herd and leave the tribe meatless. Restraint was imposed by a select society of young warriors who took over the camp when a herd was sighted and acted as policemen. They were called Dog Soldiers and they set high standards for themselves. A Dog Soldier, outnumbered,

Horse travois

would stick his staff of office into the ground and fight where he stood until he was killed or relieved.

A horse carrying a woman on his back could drag twenty-foot tent poles as travois. Several horses so burdened could transport all a family's possessions, and the tepee now became large enough for comfort. There were plenty of buffalo, so everybody had enough to eat. Why stay home and farm? Why not live where the game was? It was only necessary to dry enough meat to carry the tribe over the winter.

So, though some Indians, like the Mandan, clung to their earth-lodge villages for winter and raised a little corn, most of the farmers and woodsmen became hunters and complete nomads. No doubt the pressure of displaced tribes from the East had its part in the change, too. The farmers took their tribal customs with them and in the roaming life on the Plains one tribe learned from another, until presently there was something like a Plains way of doing things. In time, the Shoshone in the far West were following social patterns that had been folkways along the Missouri.

Tepees

The tepee was the ideal dwelling for the Plains, so everybody lived in tepees, including tribes to whom they were entirely new. White men who have lived in them say that they are the best tents in the world, warm in winter and cool in summer. They were covered with cow-buffalo hides. Ordinarily the covers were renewed each spring with skins from animals that had shed their winter coats and whose hides were thin. In June, when the tribal council was held, every band was tricked out with gleaming white tepees. By the following April the tops of the tents were completely black, shading into brown and tan toward the ground. At night the fires inside the tepees made glowing lanterns of them.

A tepee was supported by some sixteen or twenty poles, each eighteen to twenty feet long. The poles were cedar or lodgepole pine, peeled and seasoned. The tops of three poles (there was also a four-pole system) were lashed together and set up as a tripod. The lashing secured each pole

The back of a tepee.
On the ground
is a woman's saddle.

Three-pole tie
ready to be tightened and secured

it. A tepee was not a perfect cone; the poles at the back were more nearly vertical than those at the front and sides.

It took twenty or thirty tough hides sewn together to make a lodge cover. The women made a sewing bee of the job and the owner provided a feast for them. An old cover would serve as a pattern but, lacking one, the women could use the measurements of their own arms and hands and cut a tent by eye.

Several people working together could set up a tepee in three minutes. When the cover had been raised on the lifting pole, it was spread over the frame and lapped six inches down the front. This lined up the holes in both edges and they were secured together with foot-long wooden pins passed through them horizontally. The bottom of the oval door-opening was a foot from the ground and the entrance itself was three feet high. It was covered at need by a leather curtain or by an oval door of buffalo hide that was provided with loops top and bottom and was kept in shape by a couple of withes inserted in a hem. The door of a tepee faced east, away from the prevailing winds.

Attached to the front edges of the tent near its top were two smoke wings, roughly rectangular,

separately, passed twice around all three, and ended in a long line that was made fast to a ground stake inside the tent in order to anchor the structure against the wind. The rest of the poles were leaned against the tripod, their lower ends standing in an imperfect circle about sixteen feet across. The last pole was put on at the rear of the tepee and it carried the center of the cover up with

Scale of feet

Buffalo-hide tepee cover spread out flat. The dotted lines are seams.

yet with no two sides actually parallel and little more than half as wide at their bottoms as at their tops. Each wing had a hole in its top outer corner into which were inserted the extra long poles, usually crossed at the rear of the tepee, that spread the wings. Lines from the bottom corners of the wings were fastened to stakes in front of the tent. The two wings controlled the draft of the fire; the positions of the stakes and of the poles supporting the wings was governed by the direction of the wind.

When the front flaps were pinned together, the bottom ends of the frame poles were shifted outward enough to stretch the cover tightly over them. Then the lower edge of the tepee was staked down. In hot weather the edge of the cover was raised for ventilation. A lining of lightweight skins was lashed to the poles all the way around the inside of a lodge. It was about five feet high. It protected the occupants from drafts and from rain

Door of a tepee

Inside a tepee

water running down the frame poles; and the current of air that rose behind it and followed the wall upward helped keep the interior clear of smoke. In winter smoke was a secondary consideration; the space between the lining and the cover was stuffed with grass as insulation from the cold.

The women of the lodge decorated the lining with the geometric designs that were their specialty. Men usually took care of the decoration for the outsides of the lodges; they painted their totems, their exploits, and those of the tribe on them as realistically as they could, and some of their work was lively.

The inside of a tepee wasn't arranged just as a wigwam was. The fireplace was a little back of center and beds were distributed at angles to conform with the curve of the walls. Two beds on the left of the door were for the family; one on the right was for a guest. The beds were made of grass, sometimes on frames but quite often laid directly on the ground between two poles held in position by stakes. The usual skins were spread over the grass padding, and since a bed was for sitting as well as for sleep, a backrest was provided at one end. This was made of many closely spaced wil-

low sticks lashed at their ends to cords. A loop at the top served to hang the backrest on a tripod. The user kept the lower end in place by sitting on it.

Leather and Rawhide

Buffalo hide was excellent for lodges, and hides with the hair left on them made warm robes for winter use. But they were heavy and few were used for ordinary clothing if elk, antelope, or deer hides could be had. The dressing and tanning of hides by the Plains Indians followed much the same procedure that has been described for the woodlands: scraping, braining, and so on. An exception was that the stretching wasn't often done on frames; instead, the skins were pegged out on the ground.

Much use was made of rawhide that had been scraped and dehaired but not finished further. Rope for lashing tepee poles and for lariats was made of rawhide; saddles for women were covered with it. String was either rawhide or sinew, and bags made of it were used as cooking utensils. It made the soles of moccasins. Soaked in

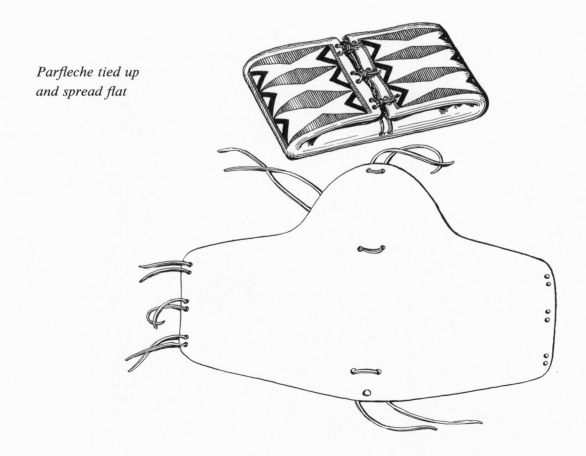

Parfleche tied up and spread flat

water and wrapped around a broken arm it would harden into a splint as rigid as one made with plaster. One of its most important uses was as material for parfleches, which were the traveling bags of the Plains. These pouches also served for storage, much as the birch-bark mocuck did in the northern woods.

A parfleche was made of a whole hide trimmed to the round-cornered shape shown in the diagram. When folded, it was fastened with rawhide lacings drawn through holes punched in the edges of the hide. Both clothing and food were kept in parfleches. Whatever was to be stored was placed on the spread-out skin; the sides were folded over it and tied in place; then the ends were brought together and tied at three points. Parfleches were almost invariably decorated with paint.

Clothing

On ordinary occasions men of the Plains dressed like other Indians; a breechclout and moccasins were enough. They seldom wore short leggings and their long, rather loose ones were usually made with wide flaps on the outside that were sometimes fringed and often heavily decorated, in early days with quillwork, later with beads. Such flaps would have been a nuisance in the woods but they gave no trouble on horseback; they were, in fact, the origin of the cowhand's leather chaps.

Moccasins stuffed with grass or hair, leggings, and a buffalo robe, worn hair-side-in, were usually enough clothes for a man in cold weather. Snow hampered buffalo, and they were often

Masculine attire

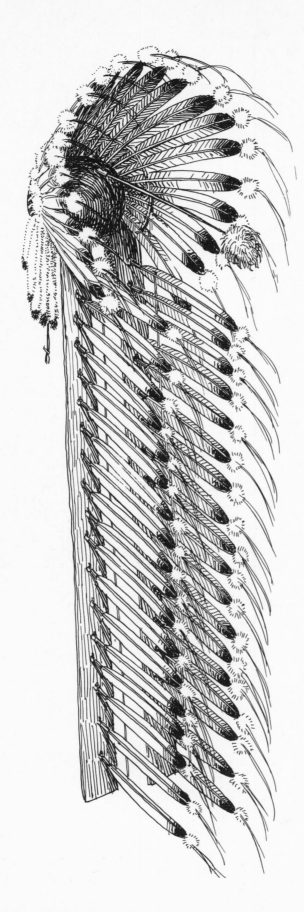

Rear view of a war bonnet with two trails

hunted on snowshoes in order to get the hides when they were most heavily coated and made warmer robes. When a woman decorated a robe she generally used the sunburst pattern that shows in the drawing on page 95, but often a warrior painted his robe with pictures of his exploits, just as he did his tepee; always sticking to the exact truth.

At times the Plainsman wore a kind of shirt made of two deer or elk skins. Originally the complete hides were used with only the hoofs removed. It was worn as a poncho and it had no sleeves. Later shirts were trimmed up more. The skins were cut straight across just back of the forelegs and the front parts were put over the shoulders as open sleeves, sewn together only at the cuffs. The legs of the skins were shortened and edges and ends were fringed. These garments were trimmed with bands of beadwork over the shoulders and down the arms; fringes of feathers or hair were attached to one edge of these bands. A standing collar of beaded leather and a breastplate made of two rows of polished bones often went on over the shirt.

Many Plains Indians wore their hair long, either braided or loose, but many tribes also had special ways of hairdressing that were peculiar to them. Roaches were worn, usually artificial ones, and no one man might wear one until he had earned the right to do so. So with eagle feathers: worn individually, each represented an exploit and was marked to designate that exploit. War-bonnet feathers weren't marked; nevertheless, when an old chief appeared with a bonnet fanning out around his head and trailing to the ground behind him, each feather in it represented one officially awarded by the tribal council. With almost no encouragement he would recount the whole saga. If he were a very great man indeed, he would be permitted to wear a buffalo-horn headdress, with his feathers arranged like a roach.

It's necessary to say here that the true war bonnet belonged only to the Plains and was worn even there by but few men. When other Indians wear them now, they do so only because it is expected of them.

A war bonnet was "big medicine"; it protected its wearer in battle, where it was the only clothing worn other than a loincloth. The bonnet was

96

made on a buckskin cap that tied on by a string under the chin. Each feather was attached by a leather loop to a lacing run around the edge of the cap. A few inches above the loops the feathers were connected by a thong that passed through all of the quills to keep them in place. Tufts of down or of white weasel fur were tied to the bases of the feathers and sometimes to their tips. The tips were further decorated with a few long strands of horsehair. One very long quill, stripped bare and tufted with an eagle plume, projected from the crown of the buckskin cap. White weasel skins, worn hanging from the sides of a war bonnet, were purely ornamental.

Just why Plains Indians needed soles on their moccasins, when they weren't needed elsewhere, isn't clear. Plains moccasins did have rawhide soles, however. They were also shaped to fit the right and left feet, and this at a time when white men were still suffering in shoes that were identical for both feet.

Except for the tongue, the upper of a Plains moccasin was a single piece of buckskin cut square across the heel end and curved around the toe. A T-shaped cut was made in it, with the stem of the T starting at the back. The tongue was attached to the cross of the T, and the two halves of the back of the shoe were joined in a vertical seam. The cuff of such a moccasin usually stood straight up; sometimes leather was added to it so that it reached well above the ankle.

The rawhide sole was cut larger than the foot outline and sewed to the upper a little above ground level. Some tribes made complete moccasins of buckskin and added rawhide soles over the buckskin ones. Dressy moccasins were often covered entirely with beads in the 19th century. This work was always completed before the sole was attached.

Women wore moccasins, short leggings and, both winter and summer, calf-length dresses made of two whole elk skins, one in front, the other behind. A separate yoke covered the chest and

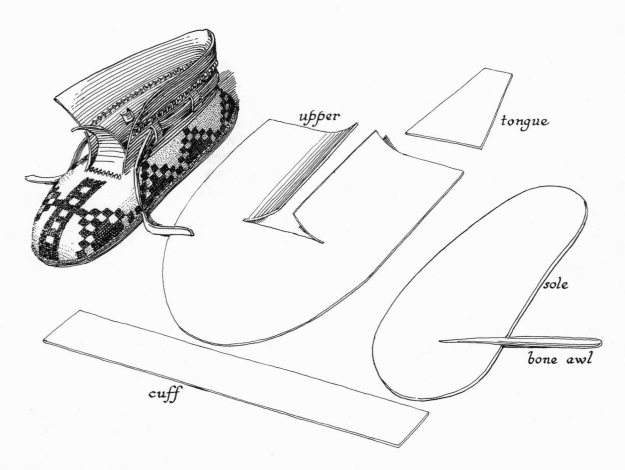

Plains beaded moccasin and its parts

Plains girl.
Her dress is ornamented with elk teeth.

the baby's head, and the side pieces of the frame extended a little below and quite a lot above the baby, looking much like a couple of fence pickets. A cradleboard shows in the travois illustration on page 90.

Beadwork

The Plains women are world famous for their beadwork and they didn't learn it from the whites; but the small porcelain and glass beads they used were made in Europe and could be obtained only through the whites. The Easterners were the first to substitute beads for the traditional porcupine quills. The Plains women didn't start using beads until 1800 and didn't get into their stride until after 1850.

Beads were sometimes "woven" into bands, using the same method that the woodland Indians used for their much coarser wampum, but as a rule, beads were sewn on buckskin, either on strips to be applied or directly on garments. Sinew was used for thread. Sewing was done by poking the sinew through holes made with a small bone awl. The beads were either strung on the stitches or strung first and sewed down with a second thread. In either case the stitches caught only an upper layer of the hide and didn't show on the underside.

The stitches for the one-thread method were placed side by side in rows with what embroiderers call "lazy stitch." The result was a pattern of parallel bands, visible in the finished work. The two-thread method produced an even surface broken only by such pattern as the beads themselves made. Being woman's work the designs used for beadwork were invariably geometrical and some of them were intricate. They were based on the old quill designs and were no improvement on the best of those.

shoulders. The dress was seamed up the sides as high as a rather wide belt that fastened at the back. The seams were fringed and so was the bottom of the skirt. Streamers of buckskin were fastened to the skirt as a rule and beadwork was distributed on the yoke and elsewhere according to tribe and taste. A completely beaded yoke, the labor of weeks, might weigh fourteen pounds. Tastefully spaced elk teeth were also admired as ornaments.

Beadwork was lavished on cradleboards, too, and some were completely covered with it. Cradleboards differed in various parts of the Plains but they usually lacked the protective hoop above

Food and Cooking

When the buffalo herds outdistanced the tribe, food was limited to the starvation point. Ordinarily, supply far exceeded demand, though nearly all of the supply was meat. When animals were killed, a small proportion of the flesh satisfied everybody's hunger; in fact, these Indians

Stone pemmican hammer.
Its rawhide jacket is shrunk on.

into pemmican, which kept very well. To make pemmican the dried meat was pounded into bits and stirred into hot fat. Wild berries were added and the whole mess was poured into a section of large intestine and tied up. White men found it repulsive but could get used to it when there was no other food to be had. White men also found that after a winter in camp they relished raw buffalo liver as much as the Indians did.

Wood was scarce in the grasslands. Dried buffalo chips (dung) were the usual fuel. These burned with a hot flame and with little smoke. Meat was broiled by holding it near the fire, impaled on a stick. It was also boiled by dropping hot stones into a vessel with it; a fair percentage of ashes went in, too. The stones were handled with tongs made from a bent sapling and shaped so much like the Southerners' lacrosse sticks that one wonders if the game didn't start from an impromptu contest with the tongs. The old midland tribes along the eastern fringe of the Plains made pottery; those on the west made baskets that they waterproofed with pitch. The Dakota and some other tribes boiled their food in buffalo stomachs or in rawhide bags.

often overate and were made ill. The rest of the meat was cut into strips, dried, and smoked. Around any camp in summer the meat-drying racks were conspicuous and full.

A buffalo was skinned and cut up where it fell. The man who killed it took the hide, the fat hump, the tongue (a delicacy), and the choicest parts of the meat. The rest was divided so that everybody had some. All of the fat was carefully kept in skin bags.

Smoked meat, almost as hard as horn, was stored in parfleches and kept pretty well even though it hadn't been salted. Some of it was made

Stone boiling

War and Magic

Because they were in the main well-fed with small effort, the Plains tribes had leisure to develop the fine points of the war game. Some of their fighting had the practical purpose of defending hunting grounds or of extending them by armed trespass, but most of it was for fun. And since it was for fun, exhibitions of foolhardy courage were held in higher esteem than the actual killing of an enemy. He who dared to strike an armed foe with his bare hand or with a harmless stick or who disarmed his enemy might "count coup," and for the rest of his life he was privileged to wear a feather that attested his deed. This was another of the midland customs that the Plains Indians took over. There were dozens of ways of counting coup. Stealing an enemy's horse from the midst of his camp would serve, or being the first to touch the body of a dead enemy even though someone else had killed him. The great Crow chief Aleek-chea-ahoosh (Plenty Coups) counted his first coup before he was nine years old when, on foot, he struck a wounded buffalo bull on the rump with his bow.

These Indians took scalps and displayed them stretched on hoops and hanging from poles in front of their tepees. Sometimes they hung them on their persons, their weapons, or their horses, but a scalp was a minor matter compared to scoring a coup. Achievement marks made with altered feathers and body paint varied from tribe to tribe, but anyone familiar with them could tell at once what a warrior's exploit had been. The marks on the legs of the Hidatsa dancers on page 20 show that they have stolen horses and have successfully attacked an enemy stronghold. The Dakota feathers shown here are only a few of many. A Dakota who informally wore a plain eagle feather horizontally in his hair had counted coup in some way. One who didn't rate such a feather was forbidden to marry until he was twenty-five years old.

Along with all this, there was much magic and "medicine" connected with war. Every man had his private medicine bundle that he carried with him for protection in battle. Like all such bundles, it contained sacred objects connected with his dreams; often the bundle itself was the skin of his totem animal. His war bonnet, if he rated one, was

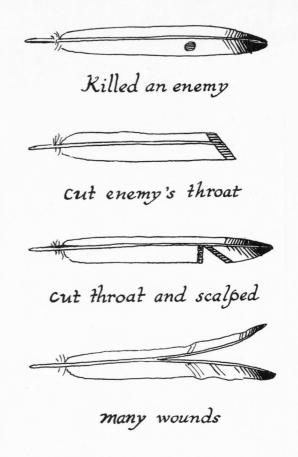

Killed an enemy

cut enemy's throat

cut throat and scalped

many wounds

Some honor feathers

a further safeguard, but his principal dependence was his shield.

It was a good practical shield made from the breast or neck hide of a bull buffalo. The raw hide was cut as a disk twice the size the shield was to be and was shrunk by steaming it over hot stones. As the hide shrank to half its original diameter, it doubled in thickness. It was dried with a slight bulge in the center, and arows were shot at it to test its resistance to puncture. Just so, in medieval Europe, armor was tested for "proof."

The hide was laced on a hoop about eighteen inches in diameter and its front surface was painted with symbols of enormous power. These were obtained in dreams. So potent were they that they were normally hidden by a decorated buckskin cover, which was removed only in battle to expose the enemy to the full glare of the medicine. The powerful symbols are not impressive, or even handsome, to the eye of a white man.

The shield hung from the left shoulder by a sling. Sometimes it was a nuisance, and when this

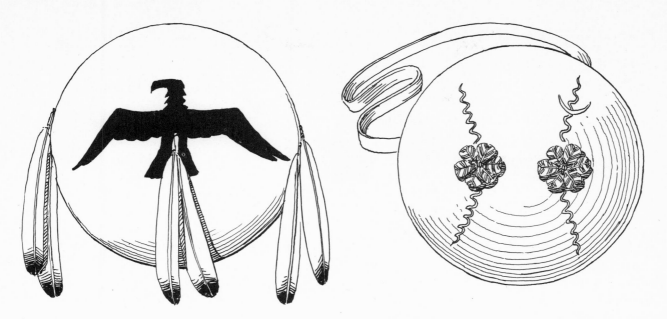

A shield covered and uncovered. The rosettes are feathers.

seemed likely, the warrior carried a miniature replica instead. The magic powers of the little shield were considered to be just as great as those of the big one. At home the covered shield and the medicine bundle hung in the tepee in bad weather; on clear days the two hung from a tripod behind the tent as a sort of rear guard. This probably worked, since enemies also believed in their power.

Weapons

The western and northern Plains tribes could get bow wood from the forests; those of the south and east traded for Osage orange (*bois d'arc*), the best bow wood in North America; but the central Plainsmen had to make out with any kind of wood they could get, even willow. This weak wood they reinforced with sinew, laid along the back of the bow where it was stretched when the bow was bent. The sinew was taken from either side of a buffalo's backbone and was soaked, pounded, and stripped thin. It was applied in overlapping layers stuck on with glue made from boiled rawhide. After the gluing, the bow and its reinforcement were lashed with bands of damp sinew that shrank tight as they dried. These bows were less than four feet long but they were more powerful than many longer, all-wood bows, *if* the weather was dry.

A sinew-backed bow and a Plains arrow

Some Plains bows were recurved; that is, their midsections curved inward toward the archer. Most bowstrings were sinew, stripped down to filaments and twisted.

Plains arrows, too, tended to be short, to make them handy on horseback. Few with stone heads are known, because these Indians traded for iron heads from quite early times, but some there are with heads of stone, bone, horn, copper, and even hard sinew that would deflect a little if it hit a rib. The heads were very small and were eared at the rear end to help the lashing hold them in place. The nock end of the Plains arrows, where the bowstring meets them, is wider than the shaft itself and is Y-shaped. One would think this might strike the bow in passing and spoil a shot. As a rule the feathers extend further along the shaft than Eastern fletching does; sometimes a full third of the arrow is feathered. Under the feathers each man marked his arrows with his own assortment of stripes so there could be no argument as to whose arrow made a kill. A curious and nearly universal characteristic of Plains arrows is the grooves, usually three of them, that run from head to feathers. Sometimes they are straight but more often they are wavy. It has been said that they were intended to represent lightning; that they were thought to make the arrows fly better; and that they were intended to make game bleed more freely. The choice is yours. The Indians must have thought them important; it took a lot of labor to put them on an arrow.

Straight, knot-free saplings for arrows were hard to find. Sticks for this purpose were made up in bundles and smoked for several weeks high up in the tepee. This seasoned them and killed any insects that might be in them. The bark was removed from each piece after it was smoked and it was straightened by being "fried," that is, the crooked areas were greased, heated, and cooled again while being held straight with a straightener. Arrow shafts were polished with grooved stones before heads and feathers were put on.

Lances were used in the Plains more frequently than elsewhere because they were a more practical weapon on horseback than on foot. At least they were more practical for hunting buffalo; their value in war is doubtful. Anyway, they made a fine thing to hang feathers and streamers on, and they added to the impressiveness of a turn-out.

Customs

Though the Plains tribes took ideas from one another, their backgrounds were different, and each tribe kept its basic structure largely intact. Hence general statements about them are subject to exceptions. Some of them held rigidly to the clan system and traced descent through the female line; others exactly reversed that, requiring marriage within the band and tracing descent through the father.

The training of boys for hunting and war was in the hands of proven warriors. Boys needed little

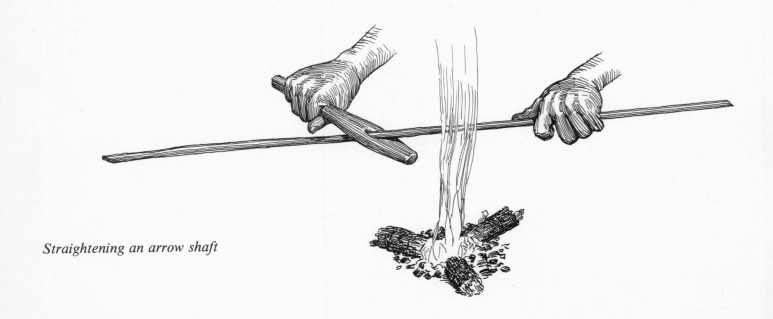

Straightening an arrow shaft

encouragement to practice horsemanship and archery, and their voluntary play was the imitation of adult heroes; but their elders also organized contests among them and instruction was given them in hunting and horse stealing. (See frontispiece.) Boys were deliberately placed in situations that would test their courage, as was the boy who struck the bull. Instruction in the tribal traditions and in sacred matters was given by the older men. Once in a while there was a failure, a boy who didn't have the stuff in him for war and hunting. For him there was no middle ground; he had to put on women's clothes and live his life as a woman.

A girl was taught by her mother, learning all the skills and duties that would fit her for the day when some young blade, wearing at least one coup feather, would pipe a love song to her on a wooden flageolet and pay her father as many horses for her as he could manage; for the number of them would be remembered and would affect her standing among the women of the tribe.

Every June the bands of each tribe gathered for a Council. The tepees were set up in four concentric rings, each band in its own established segment. In the center of the open space was the Council lodge, a tepee many times larger than a private one. It was as much as fifty feet in diameter and had no beds or other furniture in it. Here the Council "sat around in a line." They were the chiefs of all the bands, each of whom had earned his right to be there. There were no hereditary honors.

It was the task of the Council to make plans for the tribe; to receive delegations from other tribes; and to interpret the dreams of the young. The Council was the one and final court of law. Transgressors were usually sentenced to banishment. It was a harsh sentence, for an Indian, used to the interdependence of his band, was in a bad situation alone.

In the Council lodge the shaman lighted the sacred pipe with an ember and blew smoke to the earth, to the sky, and to the Four Winds; then he

Calumet

passed it to the man at the south side of the door, who puffed and passed it on. It was handed around the circle from the door to the door and back; it never crossed the opening. This was the calumet; the pipe of brotherhood; the peace pipe. It originated with the midland farmers and spread far and wide. The stem of the calumet was its sacred part; any old bowl would do. The stem was some thirty inches long and was always elaborately decorated with feathers and streamers and sometimes with the stuffed heads of ducks. The calumet was no mere symbol of peace; it had the power to *compel* peace.

Smoking wasn't confined to the peace pipe. Men and women alike enjoyed it, but young men were discouraged from indulging in it because it cut the wind. The one crop raised by all the buffalo hunters was tobacco. Women's pipes were smaller than men's and all were smaller than the calumet, except the seldom-smoked medicine pipes that men kept with their bundles. Most of the pipe bowls were made from red catlinite that came from Pipestone Quarry in the country of the Dakotas. This quarry was a sanctuary where the bitterest of enemies met in peace. It was believed to have been the scene of an ancient battle, the color of the stone resulting from the spilled blood of warriors.

There was a widespread trade in pipestone. Pipes made of it have been found many hundreds of miles from the quarry. It isn't a hard stone but it takes a fine polish. A typical Plains pipe made of it has a quite high and narrow bowl rising at a right angle from a cylindrical base that projects about half as far in front of the bowl as it does behind it. One doesn't have to be an archaeologist to see its kinship to the platform pipes of the Mound Builders.

The long stems of the Plains pipes were made of reed (*calumet* is French for reed) or of wood, with ash preferred because it had a core of pith that could be removed. There's a story that the Indians used to introduce a wood-boring worm at one end and harry him through the stem by heating the outside behind him. You may believe it, if you would like to.

A feature of the tribal powwow was likely to be the ceremony known to us as the sun dance. It was a slow stomp dance performed around a pole set up in a circular space enclosed by a token wall of brush and sometimes having a skeleton roof. The dancers fasted and abstained from drinking water before and during the dance. The idea was to continue dancing to the point of exhaustion, when one might faint and have beneficial visions. In some tribes individuals practiced self-torture as part of the ritual, to demonstrate their hardihood and to stimulate more important dreams.

Winged bone

Games

The buffalo hunters were no exception to the rule that all Indians loved games and gambling, but they seem to have had few games that were theirs alone. They played the moccasin game avidly, betting their horses and their shirts. Some of them played lacrosse and the northern ones played snowsnake, using an overhand throw that was rare in the East. Variations of snowsnake were also played with heavy-headed arrows and with "winged bones," made of feathered sections of buffalo rib.

Hoop-and-pole, the Plains version of chungke, differed from the original game. A wooden hoop replaced the chungke stone. It was usually larger than the stone and it was netted with rawhide strips, much as a snowshoe was. Most tribes rolled the hoop and tried to stop it by spearing it, sometimes counting according to the segment that was hit. A few Plains tribes tossed the hoop in the air and attacked it with pronged sticks, as in the illustration.

Plains women were devoted to a game that wasn't unknown elsewhere. It has been given the misleading name of double ball and it was almost certainly suggested by lacrosse. There was no real ball; instead, a kind of chain shot made of two

Hoop-and-pole

cylinders of rawhide connected by a thong was thrown and caught with straight sticks. Such a "ball" could be readily snared and with a little skill could be held on the stick and thrown with it. Each team tried to score goals and the players were forbidden to touch the ball. The girl on page 98 is equipped to play the game.

Communication

The many tribes of the Plains spoke widely differing languages and often even those that were related couldn't readily understand one another.

The problem of communication was solved by sign language. This remarkable system was the same for all tribes and was made up of fixed gestures to express ideas. The gestures were simple, even obvious, yet collectively they were unique. No more than examples can be given here: a stream was indicated by passing the right hand, palm down, from right to left with a wavy motion; both hands, held breast high with hanging fingers, meant rain; the same gesture, carried to the eyes, meant weep.

Each tribe had its own sign designation. Thus, the fingers of one hand, held up and moved in a shaking circle, was the Kiowa—rattlebrained; a forefinger drawn left to right across the throat was the Dakota—cutthroat. Since Indian names always made use of descriptive terms, even though they didn't describe the person, it was possible to designate individuals by sign language.

The Plainsman who wished to record events by picture writing drew upon the sign language for some of his symbols. Beside each drawing he put a dot. This was an expression of the pointed finger of a sign talker and meant, "This is it."

In addition to personal records, there are in existence a few of the winter counts that record something of the history of a whole tribe. The winter count of Wapoctaxi, a Dakota, purports to go back to the year A.D. 901! It is painted on a buffalo hide. Earlier years, held to be legendary, are dealt with in groups, each group being represented by a single symbol. From 1700 to 1880 there are symbols for every year, each illustrating one outstanding event, and they are corroborated by known facts. Some symbols record natural events, such as comets and eclipses, but many are concerned with snowy winters and shortages of food. The minor character of most Indian wars can be deduced from the fact that the killing of one man was unusual enough to serve as the designation for a whole year.

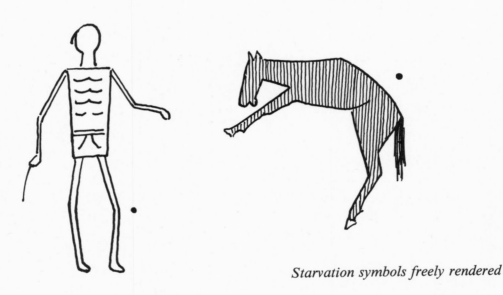

Starvation symbols freely rendered

Digger

8

West of the Rockies

In the narrow strip of land between the Sierra Nevada Mountains and the Pacific Ocean there is rainfall, but it is seasonal. East of the Sierras, in the huge area between them and the Rocky Mountains rain occurs only in occasional deluges and much of the southern end of it is true desert. Though there are hills and even mountains in it, this desert country lies generally much lower than does the land further north; hence, the north country is called the Plateau and the south, the Basin. The Indians of this whole area, from the Rockies to the sea, though they differed considerably, had one thing in common: they were all gatherers of wild food. They hunted and fished when they could, but none of them grew any crops except sometimes a little tobacco.

THE BASIN INDIANS

The people of the Basin had the hardest struggle for existence of any Indians on the continent. Once there were many lakes in the Basin but they dried up more than a thousand years ago. There's reason to suspect that the descendants of the original lake-country settlers stayed in the area after the lakes dried up, and slowly adapted themselves to the climate change. These people were bone-poor; they were primitive; they were dirty (who would waste water on washing?); and they lacked all color and dash. Other Indians and the early whites in the Basin assumed that they were inferior mentally and held them in contempt, but they were bright enough to survive in a land where a white man would, and did, starve to death.

The southern Paiute, the Bannock, and the Gosiute were typical "tribes," though they were not actually organized as tribes. It took so many square miles to provide food for each individual that these Indians had to live in small family groups, widely scattered and constantly moving. The whole preoccupation of life was survival and the people were completely realistic about it. The old and the weak who couldn't move with the group were given a little food and abandoned. It wasn't cruelty; it was stark necessity.

Gathering piñon nuts

Piñon nut
(about twice
actual size)

Food

Food was anything from which a human being could get a little nourishment. This included many wild seeds and roots, any small animals, and any insect large enough to be worthwhile. The most rewarding vegetable food was the piñon nut, the sweet seed of the piñon pine that is not disdained by modern white men. The nuts were ground into a coarse meal on stone slabs. Acorns grew in the mountains. They were ground, too, and so

were the seeds of wild grasses. Many desert plants have large fleshy roots in which they store up water and food to carry them through rainless months. The yucca is one, and there are many others. Such plants were so important to the Basin Indians that the contemptuous name for them, "Digger," came from their constant search for roots.

Jack rabbits were an important source of meat. Single rabbits were killed by throwing clubs at them, but there were also rabbit drives. Long nets made of yucca fiber were set up in sections to form a semicircle. Between each section a pit was dug, and each pit was attended by an old man armed with a club. Children fanned out for considerable distances and drove the rabbits, first into the nets and then into the pits. Another way of hunting rabbits was to encircle them by setting fire to the sagebrush and clubbing them when they had concentrated, but this had its dangers and people were sometimes burned.

Once in a great while, these Indians might come upon a herd of pronghorn antelope, and this was a glorious find. Sometimes the net trick could be worked on them. More often they were carefully

Paiute jack-rabbit roundup

Winter

stalked by hunters disguised in antelope hides and then shot with arrows at close range. To the north, where antelope were more plentiful, a shaman would sometimes betray the animals to destruction by playing upon their curiosity and leading them into a trap made of brush. Nets and antelope disguises were also used in the pursuit of sage hens. Lacking any other game—and it was often lacking —the Indians set small deadfalls for ground squirrels, gophers, and rats.

Grasshoppers and big Mormon crickets were driven into trenches from which they could be gathered in baskets. These insects were roasted until they were completely dry and then ground and stored. Snakes went into the pot whenever they were caught.

Clothing

In summer the Basin Indians needed shade, not clothes, for the weather was hot beyond all reason. Accordingly they wore as little as possible, which for men and children was ordinarily nothing whatever. The women wore aprons, made either of skins or of twine-woven strips of sagebrush bark.

Badger hide was preferred for moccasins, and sandals were woven of yucca fiber, just as the Basketmakers had made them two thousand years ago. Much that the Diggers did echoes the earliest Basketmakers, who lived in the same area. Their houses and their cradleboards were similar, and their baskets were often identical.

In winter the Basin is bitterly cold. It was then that life was hardest. It was then that desperation sometimes drove these people to eat one another. It was then that the rare owner of a buffalo robe, however bedraggled, was a rich man. Most people contented themselves with wearing the kind of woven rabbit-skin robe that has been described earlier, only here it was a rectangular cape, seldom reaching much below the hips. Men wore this garment as a tunic belted at the waist. The skins of small animals were sewn together and used as capes or were wrapped around the waist to make a kind of kilt. The hides of woodchuck, which have long fur, made a good cape. Often there wasn't enough fur of any kind and capes were made of the feathered skins of ducks. Short leggings, made by simply wrapping hides around the legs, were also worn.

Pitch-lined baskets.
A water-storage vessel, a canteen, and a stone boiler.

Baskets were made in many sizes and shapes, depending on the use for which they were intended. Large ones with wide tops were for gathering nuts and seeds. Cylindrical baskets, tarred on the inside, served as pots for boiling food with hot stones. There were even bottle-shaped baskets, also tarred inside, for carrying water. The Paiute traded baskets to the Navahos, presumably for game, since the Navahos wove no blankets until they obtained sheep from the white man.

Weapons and Ways

The scrabble for food left the Basin Indians too scattered to organize for raiding other people and they possessed nothing that made others wish to invade their inhospitable country to raid them. So as a rule they lived in peace, although they could and would fight if they had to do so. They had three-foot bows shooting arrows with stone points, and used stone-headed axes, both as tools and as weapons. When they were forced to do battle, they also carried very long spears.

There were no clans in the Basin and no marriage taboos. There was little religion beyond superstition and magic. Individuals became shamans as a result of powers that they believed some animal conferred upon them in a dream. These shamans performed tricks to gain respect and undertook to treat disease by "sucking out" the cause. Some actual object was displayed after the

Dwellings

The conical huts thatched with brush or grass that these people built were very like the huts of the earliest Basketmakers, and in winter the Diggers put their wickiups over pits for additional warmth, just as the Basketmakers did. It's probable that hut poles were taken along when the family moved; poles were scarce and it is known that the dog travois was used in the Basin.

Crafts

The Basin Indians made excellent nets for their game-catching drives. They were also very good basket makers, and some of them made a little crude pottery. Weaving seems to have been limited to aprons and rabbit-skin capes. These were often woven on the ground with no frame to hold the warp. When a frame was used, it was simply two parallel poles lashed to short stakes, which elevated them a few inches off the ground.

Some Basin baskets were twined but most were made by the coiling method, as were many other Indian baskets. Such a basket was started in the center of its bottom with a small button made by coiling yucca fiber and sewing it. Around the button a "rope" of grass, created as the work progressed, was coiled spirally and sewn in place with yucca fiber. The stitches didn't penetrate the coils, but enclosed them and passed between them. Each stitch passed around two coils: the one that was already in place and the new one that was being added. The coils of a finished basket were often covered entirely by closely spaced stitches.

Part of an unfinished coiled basket. The stitches at the left of the awl are separated to show the grass coils.

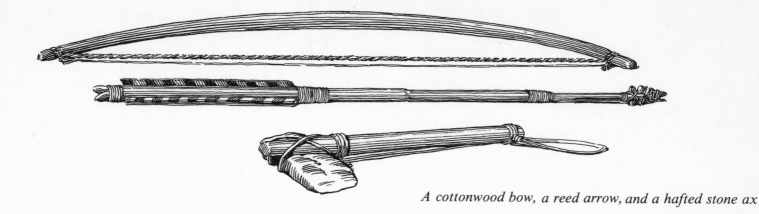

A cottonwood bow, a reed arrow, and a hafted stone ax

operation as "proof" of its success. If the patient died despite the treatment, the medicine man's own life was in some danger.

The Basin Indians had an intense superstitious fear of the dead and of anything connected with the deceased. In consequence they ordinarily placed a man's body in his wickiup along with everything he had owned and burned the whole thing. For a considerable period after that it was considered dangerous to mention his name. This was a nuisance because names were made up of words in common use and those words had to be dropped.

THE PLATEAU INDIANS

North of the Basin, in what is now Idaho, western Montana, eastern Oregon, and Washington, the land is higher and the living was easier. Basically it was the same kind of living as in the Basin but food was in better supply and other things were added to it. These were much the same kind of people, too; the only differences between them and the Basin people were those created by a more abundant diet and a little leisure. There was a wider variety of game. A hunter, wading in neck-deep water with his head covered by a large gourd, could seize the feet of a swimming duck and pull it under without disturbing the rest of

Camass

the flock. Antelope and bighorn sheep were fairly plentiful and these, in addition to providing food, gave the northerners more hides for clothing. Dress was similar to that in the Basin, but there was more of it. One article not found elsewhere was a closefitting hat of basketry worn by the women.

Submarine duck hunting

Netting salmon

camass and they called *quamash.* Then, too, the Snake River and the Salmon River, both tributaries of the Columbia, penetrated to the western foothills of the Rockies; in the spring, salmon fishing in them was as good as hope could ask.

When the salmon ran upstream to spawn, whole tribes turned out to catch them with dip nets, with seines, in fish traps, and by spearing. They were dried and smoked in such quantity as to provide a basic food supply for a whole year. These Indians (and others farther downstream) built rather fragile platforms far out over the rushing water. They balanced precariously on the tips of these and dipped big nets with curious triangular handles, bringing them up heavy with big flopping fish. Spearing was done from similar perches with three-pronged leisters.

Some of these people needed boats. In country where trees were large enough, they made dugouts. One tribe, the Kutenai, made bark canoes with exaggerated back-slanting bows, like the ram bows of 1898 battleships. Where trees were scarce, bundles of tule rushes were used to make rafts with one pointed end. Skin coracles were also built. These had rounded ends but their sides were straight, so they were just that much better than the bull boats of the upper Missouri River.

Not far from the Kutenai, in southern Canada, lived the Salishan tribes, speaking a language that has no traceable connection with any other Indian speech. They were often called the Flatheads for the reason that they let their children's heads grow naturally. Their neighbors to the west made a practice of binding boards to the heads of babies so that they grew distorted into quite notable points. Some other Indians—the Chinook for instance—were also called Flatheads, but it was because they did flatten the fronts of their heads.

The northern Shoshone, the Nez Percé, and some other tribes obtained horses and were transformed into reasonable facsimiles of Plains Indians. They hunted buffalo, which roamed far into western Montana. The western Shoshone and the northern Paiute continued in the old ways, living in pit houses and gathering seeds and roots. Even so, they were better off than the Basin people.

For one thing they could dig any quantity of the sweet edible bulbs of a lily-like plant that we call

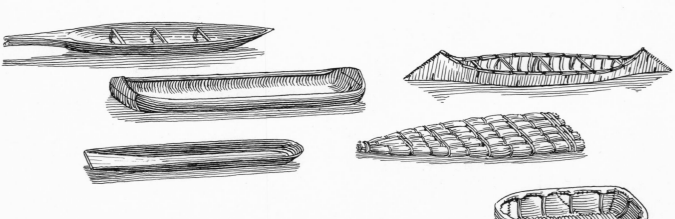

Inland boats of the Northwest:
Three dugouts, a canoe, a tule raft, and a skin coracle

Large Pomo basket

CALIFORNIA INDIANS

Scattered thickly along the coast of California there were literally dozens of small bands of Indians, all with a seed-and-root basis of life which was augmented in some cases by fish and shellfish. All but three of the known American languages were spoken by one or another of these bands, and there was one language, the Penutian, that was spoken nowhere else. It has been suggested that most of these bands were refugee remnants of tribes who, reaching the ocean, could go no further.

The main food of these Indians was acorns. These they stored in the shell and used as needed. Acorns are bitter with tannic acid; to make them edible it was necessary to crush them into meal and then to pour water through the meal until the tannin was leached out. The leaching was done in porous baskets over sand pits. Ultimately the meal was boiled as mush and was nutritious though practically tasteless.

The weather was never very cold along the coast, so clothes and houses were a minor matter. A few strings hung from a waistband or a skin worn as a kilt made a complete costume. Much of the time people did very well dressed just as nature made them. Houses were mere huts rudely thatched with bundles of rushes and looking quite a lot like neglected haystacks.

Because of their diversity, these Indians are an ethnologist's delight; but because of their sedentary dullness they aren't very interesting to the rest of us, except for a few special items: some of them made yew bows that were wide and rather flat and of such excellence that modern archers have adopted their best features. One tribe, the Pomos, made baskets that were possibly the finest ever made in the world. They were very beautiful and many of them were made so finely that they were watertight without any treatment with pitch. They were not coiled baskets; they were woven. One rather large California tribe, the Chumash, being short of trees, split driftwood into thin planks. They drilled holes along the edges of these and sewed the boards together into large canoes. The seams were made watertight with asphalt. These were the only plank boats built by any American Indians.

Chumash plank canoe

Adobe pueblo.
A kiva is in the foreground.

9

The Desert Townsmen

The pueblos of today are scattered from north-central Arizona eastward and northeastward, almost to the northern border of New Mexico. They're not all alike. Some of them are built on high mesas and some are in flat country and along rivers. On the heights they are built with stone and in the lowlands they are made of adobe mud. Most of them have been where they are for centuries and many old ones have been abandoned. The Pueblo people differ, too; they speak four unrelated languages, but there is enough similarity in their ways to indicate that they all learned pueblo living from the same source.

Most of the pueblos were built in the old step design of Pueblo Bonito, with each floor set back by the depth of one room from the front of the floor below it. None of them followed the semicircular plan of Pueblo Bonito, however. Some were built along two sides of a street; some around rectangular courts, the houses receding upward from the court, the outside walls unbroken; and some, like Taos, were built as stepped pyramids.

In all of the pueblos the lowest level was originally without doors in its walls; and in all of them the various levels were reached by ladders or notched poles that could be drawn up for defense. Without exception, the towns had some form of the kiva, the underground room that was at once a temple and a men's club. The origin of the kiva was the pit house of the Basketmakers.

Taos is the easternmost and also the northernmost of the pueblos and is still occupied. Though it holds off from the ways of the white man, it is also far from the old Pueblo ways. It had a long association with the Plains Indians and adopted many of their traits. Most of the other pueblos in New Mexico have been in close contact with white men for 300 years, and their lives and customs

114

have been changed by the experience. It was in Arizona among the Hopi and the Zuñi that the old ways of life were preserved long enough for white students to learn something about them.

The Hopi are the main source of what is given here. They spoke a language that was remotely connected with that of the Aztecs in Mexico. This doesn't mean that they were a branch of that tribe and it doesn't, in itself, connect American Indian life with that of the Aztec. There was some Mexican influence on the Hopi, but other American tribes having little or no trace of Pueblo ideas —the Kiowa, the Paiute, and the Shoshone, for instance—spoke related languages.

The Hopi still occupy three high mesas in Arizona where they have six towns, plus a seventh occupied by a band of Tewa who have lived with the Hopi for two hundred years. This town, Hano, on the farthest mesa east, is twenty miles from Oraibi, the westernmost pueblo. The 400-foot-high mesas can be reached only by narrow trails, sometimes so steep that foot- and handholds have had to be cut in the rock walls, and the springs are all at the bottoms of the hills! Generations of Hopi women slung big jars in blankets and carried every drop of household water up the trails on their backs. Centuries ago houses were built below the mesas near the springs. They were moved up for safety from the attacks of marauding Apaches.

Every Hopi pueblo had its ceremonial dance court, sometimes entirely surrounded by buildings, sometimes on the edge of a cliff. Each clan occupied a fixed section of the pueblo and allotted houses to its families according to their size. Houses were seldom more than three stories high; they were stepped back, with the ground floor and the back rooms of upper floors windowless and used for storage. Ladders were used to reach the

Water supply

roofs of the lowest level. Some ladders were used on the second level, too, but access to the top story was often by way of a narrow stair built as part of a second-floor wall. The roof of the ground floor made an excellent terrace for loafing. Much household work was done on the roofs.

Houses

The Spanish taught the New Mexican Indians of the lowlands to cast large "bricks" of adobe, dry them, and build them into walls. Before the Spanish came, the builders shaped the mud into pillow-like lumps by hand and plastered them into a wall with quantities of the same mud. The surface was slicked up with a thin coat of more mud, and this they renewed every year or so. Sometimes they built forms of poles and skins and filled them with mud that dried in them, much as concrete is poured into wooden forms today. Aside from the wall material, the lowland houses didn't differ much from the stone ones on the heights.

The mesas themselves are almost entirely stone. It isn't excessively hard and it lies in flat layers

Hopi pueblo

Edge of the mesa. A natural crevice has been walled in to save labor in excavating the kiva.

with seams of clay between them; so the principal building material was never difficult to get. The House Priest was the official architect. Call him Chief, if you like; it is only a matter of translation. He paced off the plan and placed an eagle feather under each cornerstone. Work wasn't begun without due ceremony. Bread crumbs and tobacco were sprinkled all the way around the site to the accompaniment of a song so old its words had lost all meaning. An offering of food was placed outside and inside the place where the door would be.

The men helped to quarry and sometimes helped in placing the larger stones, but most of the building was done by the women, dubiously assisted by the children. House walls were about seven feet high and averaged nineteen inches thick. The stone was laid in mud mortar and was plastered over with mud inside and out. The quality of the stonework didn't approach that of Pueblo Bonito. Foot-square windows were set high in the wall. They were sometimes filled with sheets of gypsum which, although it is not transparent, would let in a little light. The floor was mud mixed with sand and was rubbed with a smooth stone to give it finish.

Wood lasts almost indefinitely in that dry climate, so as many roof beams as possible were salvaged from ruined houses. New ones were obtained from trees that grew in gullies in the lowlands some distance away; it was men's work to

get them and carry them home. Beams were cut according to measurements provided by the House Priest. Roofs were nearly flat. Light poles were placed across the beams, with brush and grass added as the next layer, and mud over that. Spouts extended over the walls to carry off rainwater, but all of the roofs leaked in a hard rain.

Originally, there were few doors in any walls. One entered a house by climbing a ladder to the roof and descending another that projected through the smoke hole. After the Spanish came, smoke holes were replaced by small corner fireplaces with chimneys made from stacks of old pots with their bottoms knocked out; after that, houses had doors. Because wood is scarce on the mesas, the Hopi once burned coal and are the only Indians known to have done so.

The dark back rooms of the houses were used to store corn in stacks according to color: red, yellow, white, blue, black, and parti-colored. The family lived in the one front room, which was not very large. A suspended pole served as the only place to store clothes and blankets; a small shelf built into the wall was the pantry. There were several water jars in the room and near one wall there were three flat stones for grinding corn: one coarse, one medium, and one fine. By the fire there was a smooth stone that could be heated for cooking. There were no beds; at night blankets were spread informally on the floor.

The People of Peace

In their own language the Hopi are the *Hopitu,* the Peaceful Ones. This is literally descriptive. Unlike other Indian farmers, the Hopi made no cult of war and wouldn't fight except in defense of their homes, which they were sometimes compelled to do because their homes were bait for the Apache. The Hopi were the most urbane of all American Indians; they were good-humored and cheerful, the women jolly. They were imaginative and clever people, sharp traders, and skilled craftsmen. Their manners were excellent and their children, though seldom punished, were well-behaved. Lest they sound like paragons, it must be said that, though the Hopi were sometimes neat, they were seldom clean.

These Indians weren't real sports devotees, and they seem to have had no games that were theirs

Pueblo interior

alone. Even their foot races, though they were enjoyed as sport, had a religious motive; that of rounding up the gods and herding them nearer to the town. Most athletic contents were casual and spontaneous. The same attitude applied to sedentary games; their version of the moccasin game, played with pottery bowls, was for amusement only. Here were Indians with little or no interest in gambling, the only ones of their kind.

The men weren't very tall but they were well-built, agile, and graceful. Their phenomenal endurance as runners has been mentioned earlier. The Hopi had brown skins and straight black hair. Men wore it either in a queue bound up in the back or in the long bob they inherited from the Basketmakers. Heads were artificially flattened at the back by binding them to the cradleboard in infancy. The Hopi nose is broad and rather flat. There is a bony ridge above the eyes, and the eyes themselves, though not large, show little or no slant. The mouth is large and full and the whole expression of the face is open and pleasant; this may be said about few Indians.

In spite of toting fifty-pound loads of water up a 400-foot cliff daily, Hopi women were often a bit more than pleasingly plump. No other Indian women paid as much attention to hairdressing as they did. The hair of marriageable girls was dressed in two big buns standing away from the sides of the head. These were intended to represent squash blossoms. The hairdress was changed

117

at marriage; it was wrapped into two pendant clubs, which represented squash fruits.

Clothing

In early times the Hopi wore sandals woven of yucca fiber or cut from rawhide. When they found that moccasins were better than sandals for running, they adopted them. Their moccasins were much like those of the Plains Indians. A woman's moccasins required a whole deerhide, cut in half diagonally. These were really moccasins plus leggings, most of the hide being wrapped around the lower leg until it looked as thick as a stovepipe. Every bride had to have a pair of these, and they are still worn on formal occasions, though not so frequently by the Hopi as by the Zuñi and the

Coiffeurs, maiden and matron

*Hopi couple
in the old costumes*

pueblos to the east. In daily life most Hopi women went barefoot.

Pueblo men of today wear trousers and shirts but their ancient costume appears at ceremonies: a white kilt held in place by a richly ornamented and colored sash. Often an animal pelt hangs from the sash at the back. Formerly, they wore many necklaces made of shells and colored stones; the wearing of a woven headband just above the eyebrows still persists.

The women of old time wore cotton dresses made blue with dye extracted from sunflower seeds. The dress was made from a hand-woven rectangle. Two corners were joined on the right shoulder, and the edges on that side were fastened together from under the arm to the bottom. The left shoulder was bare. The dress reached a little below the knee. It was held in at the waist by a narrow sash of many colors that was wrapped around the body several times.

In cool weather both sexes used cotton blankets worn over the shoulders, like a shawl, or sometimes over the head. It can get pretty cold on the mesas and when it did the inevitable rabbit-skin blanket appeared. Shirts of antelope hide with

long tails behind weren't unknown for men. Children dressed like their elders when they dressed at all, which was only in cold weather.

Farming

From the earliest time that anything is known about the Pueblo Indians they have been town-dwelling farmers and they have successfully farmed some of the least likely land in the world. The mesas of the Hopi are surrounded by the Painted Desert and in it they have their fields, some of them twenty miles from home.

The Pueblo people learned how to make the desert yield crops hundreds of years ago; they had to do it or die. They discovered that water accumulated underground in low spots and that the roots of their plants could reach it. They found out where the courses of underground streams lay and made fields over them. They learned, too, that desert-growing plants need more room than they would need in a moister climate, so their corn hills were spaced ten feet or more apart.

Pueblo men did the farming. Probably one reason they were so little interested in fighting was that they couldn't be spared from the fields. The old men helped with weeding and the old women and the children worked at scaring off crows. The whole process of "plowing" and cultivating was done with a single implement, a digging stick about four-and-a-half feet long on which the stump of one branch had been left a few inches from the bottom. This allowed the foot to help in digging.

Squash, gourds, tobacco, and several kinds of beans were grown. There were cotton fields, too,

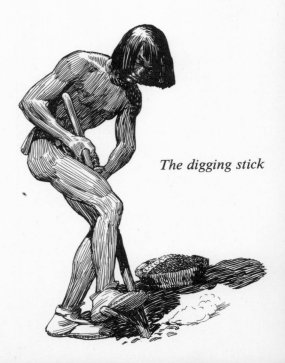

The digging stick

the only ones in North America. There is a wild cotton native to this country but this wasn't it. This was domestic American cotton; botanists can duplicate it only by crossing native wild cotton with the domestic cotton of Asia. This has aroused speculation. It seems highly unlikely that any prehistoric immigrant crossed the Bering Straits with a pocketful of cotton seed.

As everywhere in America, corn was the chief crop, and the Pueblos grew excellent corn in their dry wastelands. In more productive areas the Indians sowed four grains to a hill and thinned it after it had a good start; the Pueblo men planted twenty grains to a hill and didn't thin it at all! Their growing corn looked quite different from corn elsewhere in America. A hill of it gave the appearance of a low bush; its ears had learned to huddle near the ground, under the leaves and out of the blaze of the sun.

Grinding

Pueblo corn

Storing and Grinding Corn

Feasts of green corn were held, but most of the corn was husked and carefully dried for storage by being hung in bunches from the houses. In desert country the air is so dry that it sucks the moisture out of anything in short order. The storage of corn, grinding it into meal, and cooking it were women's jobs. They often ground corn together in groups of three, singing and chattering all day long and powdering their faces with meal to absorb perspiration. The three women would work side by side, each using a stone of different fineness. The stone was a flat slab, now called by

119

its Spanish name *metate*. The grinding was done by rubbing the grains across it with another stone, the *mano*, held in the hands. The stone of the metate was soft and it gradually wore away, becoming thin in the middle. It is still a standing joke in the area that every man has to eat a metate in his lifetime.

Cooking

The Pueblos knew fifty-two ways of cooking corn. Most of them weren't unlike the ways other Indians cooked it, but the "paper bread," called *piki,* belonged to them alone. It was made from a thin batter and was cooked on a flat stone placed over the fire. The batter was colored—sometimes red, sometimes yellow—for special feasts, but ordinarily it was gray because wood ashes were deliberately mixed with the meal.

Dexterity was needed in a good piki maker. The stone was greased and smoking hot. The cook dipped her hand in the batter and with a gesture that had to be quick to save her from blisters spread the batter thinly and evenly over the stone.

Cooking piki

Eagle trap

Cooking was nearly instantaneous. Usually piki were folded into neat rectangles as soon as they were cooked. The gray ones looked exactly like the paper of which a hornet's nest is made, but they have been reported as delicious.

Weapons and Hunting

The Hopi made good sinew-backed bows and at least two kinds of arrows: a short, quite thin, wooden one and a much longer reed arrow with a wooden foreshaft and a notched stone head. Each type was suited to special uses. In pre-Spanish days there were fair supplies of game near the mesas. Pronghorn antelope were the most important game but the Hopi occasionally took deer, mountain lions, and even buffalo.

They were never above the pursuit of rabbits, both cottontails and jacks. For this they depended on their abilities as runners and were armed only with the Pueblo "boomerang," or throwing stick. This was a curved stick the design of which evolved from Basketmaker days. In appearance and size it was quite like the boomerang of the Australian bush, though it had none of that weapon's remarkable tricks. Nevertheless, it was a good weapon and the Pueblo people killed quantities of rabbits with it.

Though secondary to agriculture, hunting was important to the diet of these Indians. After the large game was gone, rabbits, ground squirrels, and sage hens were the main sources of meat. Still

later, a sheep, a burro, or a horse might vary the menu. From earliest times, it is also likely that dogs occasionally went into the pot.

Domestic Animals

The Pueblo Indians had two kinds of dogs. One kind was small, short-bodied and sturdy, with short legs and a short, broad nose; quite possibly it was short-haired, too, and it was either all black or black and white. It had the erect ears that almost all Indian dogs had. The other dog was somewhat larger and more slender in build. It had a weak, bushy tail that was rather short and gave the impression of being fat under its hair. These larger dogs had long, thick coats that were yellowish on the back, brown on the head and ears, and white on the throat and belly. They were regularly sheared by their owners and the hair was spun and woven.

Wild turkeys were tamed and domesticated by the Pueblos, partly for food but more importantly for their feathers. The costumes and properties used in Pueblo religious ceremonies demanded lots of feathers. Eagles were kept in sullen captivity as another source of supply.

The Indian method of catching eagles is worth mention; it wasn't confined to this one area. A man-sized pit was dug and covered with poles and brush, and a dead animal was tied on top of it as bait. When an eagle landed at the lure, the hunter hidden in the pit reached up and grabbed it by both legs. One hopes the hunter had an assistant with him, because merely having a grip on the legs of an adult eagle doesn't mean that you have captured it!

Baskets

All of the Pueblo Indians once made baskets but most of them have now abandoned the craft. As with many other old ways, the Hopi and the Zuñi kept the craft alive and still make some very fine baskets. Regardless of the materials and the methods used in making them, most Pueblo baskets were of two shapes: they were flat trays, for meal, or deep storage baskets with lids. The kind of bowl-shaped basket with a wide top that is handy for gathering seeds was made, too, but less frequently.

Rabbit stick

The Hopi on two of the three mesas specialized in basketry and each group had its own method of making them. Those on the middle mesa made coiled baskets in a manner similar to the Paiute way that has been described, but the grass coils were much thicker and the yucca-fiber stitches were put through the coil itself, not just around it. The stitches completely covered the surface of the finished basket.

Yucca fibers were dyed in various colors by boiling them with roots, flowers, seeds, or minerals and then smoking them to set the color. The dyed fibers were used to make decorations on the baskets. This took careful planning and stitch counting. The planning was all mental; there was no pattern; the design grew with the basket. All of the ornaments are said to represent natural objects and some of them obviously do, but many of them were so conventionalized that they were merely geometric shapes.

The western mesa made—and still makes—wicker baskets, using willow or sumac withes for warp and weaving them together with flexible material from several plants known collectively as "rabbit brush." The weaver starts by placing a number of the withes side by side as warps, few for a small basket, more for a large one. Rabbit brush is used to weave a flat, square mat on the withes halfway between their ends. Two such mats are placed one over the other, with the withes at right angles, and are tied together at their corners. The warps are then spread apart so that they radiate like the spokes of a wheel, and the weaving begins.

The work proceeds in a continuous spiral gradually becoming circular as it moves outward from the square base. After a few turns, the warps, spreading as they do, are too far apart; more are added by merely thrusting the ends of them into the completed fabric. When the basket reaches its finished size the warps are bent sideways and are lashed together with yucca fiber to form a rim. Ornamentation may be woven into such a basket with pre-dyed material or it may be painted on the finished product with a rabbit-hair brush. Indians like bright colors, and now that they can get them, they use them; but almost none of the pigments they once got from natural sources were brilliant.

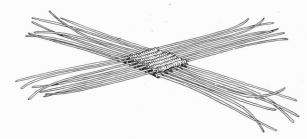

The start of a wicker basket

Pottery

Sedentary agricultural Indians were always more interested in making clay pots for themselves than were the hunters who had to move about a lot; pots were heavy and easily broken. All of the Pueblo Indian women made pottery and most of them still do so, for the reason that it is readily saleable to tourists. Curiously, the Hopi no longer make pottery, though the Tewa band that lives with them does make it. The modern shapes of Pueblo pottery have been influenced by the tourist trade. The old shapes, though beautiful, were dictated by practical needs. They were water-

Wicker basket-making.
The position of the worker's legs
was the customary one
with Pueblo women.

Tewa pottery from Hano pueblo

storage jars, canteens, bowls, and cooking pots.

The method of making them applies with few variations to Indian potters anywhere on the continent. The clay, dug wherever a good deposit could be found, was dried, pounded, and culled of all foreign matter. Then it was tempered by mixing in a little sand to keep it from cracking when it was fired. Water was added after the tempering, and the mass was kneaded to smoothness.

The potter's workbench was the ground or the floor of her house. She had no potter's wheel to help in making the work symmetrical. Some sort of working base was used: an old meal tray, the bottom of a broken pot, or a flat stone. On the base the potter patted a "pie" of clay. This was the bottom of the new piece; its edge was turned up a little all the way around, so clay could be added to it to build the pot to its final form.

If the article was a small one, rings of clay were made and pressed on successively, one on top of another. For a large vessel clay rolls were formed between the palms and added to the wall spirally, much as a coiled basket was made. The coiled wall wasn't completed in the rough and then given its finished shape; it was shaped as it went along, a couple of inches at a time. Very large jars had to be partially dried at intervals so the wall would be strong enough to support clay that was added to it. When this was done the upper edge was kept moist to make sure that new clay would stick to it.

The work was turned constantly and was shaped with tools made of pieces of dried gourd. Wherever the tool was pressed against the clay it was backed up, on the other side of the flexible wall, by the potter's fingers. If the pot was to have handles, holes were made for them. The handles were formed from rolls of clay that were thrust through the holes and smoothed out on the inside. A very small pot could be shaped in ten minutes; a large one took as much as six hours.

Clay can't be fired until it is completely dry, and if it dries too fast it's apt to crack, so the Pueblo pots were dried in the shade or indoors. Small cracks could be repaired; a large one ruined the pot. When the work was dry it was carefully scraped all over the outside with the sharp edge of a stone or with a piece of broken pottery. A common cooking vessel was then ready for firing, but any fancier article was given two or three coats of slip. This was clay made very thin with water and it was spread on with a bit of fur. Often the slip was different in color from the pot itself; red clay might be slipped with white. The final coat of slip was polished with a smooth stone when it had dried. This was not a glaze.

Ornamentation was painted freehand on the slip with brushes cut from yucca leaves and frayed at one end by chewing. Most of the colors—yellows, dull reds, and browns—were colored earths. Black was iron or manganese. The minerals were powdered in stone mortars and mixed with water.

When she had an accumulation of dry pots on hand, the potter started a fire in her kiln, which was simply a shallow depression filled with the ashes of old fires that was located where the wind wouldn't hit it. Her wares were set around the edge of the kiln and were warmed and further dried as the fire caught up. Presently, the fire was raked aside and the pots placed in the middle of the pit upside down, their rims resting on stones. Small articles were often covered with big ones, but no pot was allowed to touch another. Flat

Potter

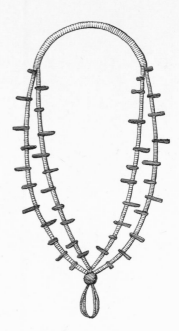

Pueblo shell-and-turquoise necklace

stones and large shards of old pots were stood on edge around the collection to keep the fire from getting too close to the pottery and blackening it.

The fire was raked against this wall all the way around and fuel was built up on it until it formed a dome over the whole firing. The object was to make the dome burn on the inside, and to that end, fuel was added to cover any holes that burned through. People near the firing were required to speak in whispers, because loud talk would cause the spirits in the pots to break them. The heat was intense, as much as 1,500 degrees, and it was kept up for a couple of hours. When the fire died down, the pots were raked from the ashes and, still pretty hot, were dusted off. They were ready for use as soon as they had completely cooled.

Jewelry

There are now excellent Pueblo silversmiths but the art was learned after the Spanish showed the Indians what silver was. Much turquoise is used with the silver. Pueblo craftsmen have always had this material, but not very much of it and only within the last half century have they imported it from Asia. The old artisans did import shells, however, from California and from the Gulf Coast. These they added to native stones to make the great variety of double and triple necklaces that everybody wore.

Small shells were drilled and strung as they were, or they were trimmed a little to make them look better. Large shells, chiefly abalone, were broken into small fragments. These were pierced with a bow drill and strung in short lengths so tightly that the irregular bits were pulled into a nearly rigid column. This was then rolled between two slabs of sandstone, and the bits of shell were quickly ground into smooth cylinders of uniform size. Turquoise beads were made the same way, but the grinding took longer because turquoise is much harder than shell. Beads of irregular shape were often strung with the others for variety.

Weaving

Navaho Indian women have become justly famous as weavers of blankets but all that they know of the craft they learned from the Pueblos. The Hopi men, for it is they who do most of the weaving, can still outdo them. The ancient Hopi wove the cotton they grew and also added to it rabbit fur, dog hair, feathers, and probably buffalo wool. Their cotton was cleaned of seeds by hand and was worked into condition for spinning by whipping it with switches on beds of sand. It was spun into yarn on hand spindles not essentially dif-

The Hopi loom

ferent from those used in Asia and North Africa.

The Pueblos were the only Indians in North America who used a loom. It was crude, even by comparison with the hand looms of the early white settlers, but it was a true loom. Warp threads were stretched on it and alternate ones could be moved in unison, so as to open what weavers call "sheds." The Hopi loom was strung vertically between two stout horizontal poles: one suspended above, often from the projecting ends of roof beams against a wall, the other held on the ground by pegs or weights. Lashed to the upper side of the bottom pole was a lighter parallel pole, called a yarn beam, to which the lower ends of the warps were attached. There was an upper yarn beam, too, but it wasn't hung directly from the upper pole of the loom; instead, it was lashed to a second light pole which, in turn, was laced to the top pole. This lacing was continuous and served to tighten the warp.

The work of stringing the warp, a vital part of weaving, wasn't done directly on the loom. It was easier to remove both yarn beams and use them as the temporary ends of a rectangular frame laid flat on the ground. The warp was strung on this as a continuous thread passing around both yarn beams and stretching between them in evenly spaced lines. The thread was always taken *over* both beams so that, viewed from one end, the warp described long figure eights and so formed two ready-made sheds, one above and one below the crossing point. These sheds were maintained throughout the weaving.

The weaver didn't dare cut the warp, because he wanted two ravel-proof ends to his work. So he made them while the warp was still on the temporary frame by hand-twilling three cords across the outer ends of the warps where they passed over the beams. Twilling is weaving by skipping over two or more warps and passing under only one. Slender rods were put into the two sheds to hold them and to keep the warps from tangling, and then the warp beams were removed and tied in place, bare, on the loom.

The warp was laced to the beams with cords that engaged the twilled bands at its ends.

When the warp was tightened with the top lacing, its two sheds almost vanished and were kept in existence only by the rods that had been put into them. The upper rod remained where it was, keeping the upper shed always slightly open, until the fabric was woven so close to it that it had to be removed. The lower one was left in place only until the heddles, which took over the job of opening the lower shed, could be attached to the warp threads. The heddles were loops of a continuous cord, with each loop passing behind a warp thread and around a rod that lay in front of the whole warp. When the heddle rod was pulled forward, it moved with it the threads to which it was looped; that is, every other warp thread, all that belonged to the lower shed. By using two or more of these heddle rods, the Hopi were able to weave patterns. Each rod controlled selected parts of the shed.

Weaving began at the bottom of the frame. The shuttle was nothing more than a short stick with a few turns of weft yarn wound on it. Even so, it was too bulky to pass through the narrow slot of either shed, so the weaver resorted to his batten. This was a thin wooden slat a couple of feet long. Turned on edge, it slipped readily into the shed slot, and when rotated a quarter turn, it opened the shed wide. The shuttle could be passed only the length of the batten. If the fabric was wider than that length, the batten had to be inserted from both sides or even slipped in between two warp threads.

The upper shed, held slightly open by its rod, extended all the way to the bottom of the warp. Its threads stood a little in front of those of the lower shed and passed between the rather loose loops of the heddles. The opening was wide enough to permit the insertion of the batten into the upper shed *below* the heddle rod. The first weft was put in and pushed down tight with the edge of the batten and with a comblike affair called the reed fork. For the next weft the weaver pulled the

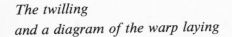

*The twilling
and a diagram of the warp laying*

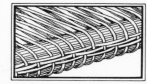

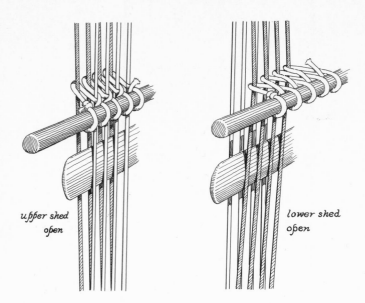

The mechanics of the Hopi loom

heddle rod toward him, bringing the lower shed far enough in front of the upper to admit the batten. Each new weft was pressed tightly into place, and as the cloth grew, the heddle rod was slid upward. This wasn't a fast way to weave but it was ever so much faster than dealing with one warp thread at a time as other Indians did, and the quality of the weaving could be as good as anything the white man's loom produced.

As work on the fabric progressed upward it presently reached an awkward height for weaving. When that happened the lacing at the top of the frame was loosened and a fold was taken in the lower part of the cloth. This was carefully sewn down. When the top lacings were tightened again, the working area was in easy reach. It was the last few inches that gave trouble on this kind of loom. After the work had progressed so far that the batten couldn't be inserted, the passage of the shuttle slowed up; when the top shed rod came out, it all but stopped. Finally it did stop entirely, and the last wefts between the edge of the finished web and the top twilling were poked in with a pointed stick.

The elaborately patterned sashes of the Hopi were made on a loom that worked the same way, though it was used horizontally. It was narrow to correspond with the work, and it had several heddle rods for the weaving of the patterns. Everything else was simplified; the batten reached clear across the web and a single blow of the reed fork would compact a weft the full width of the sash.

125

Government

There was no one headman in a pueblo; power was vested in a council in which sat the chiefs of the clans and the priest-chiefs: the House Priest, the Sun Priest, the Kiva Priest, the War Chief, and the Speaker.

The Sun Priest kept the calendar for ceremonies. He watched the horizon and noted where the sun rose and set behind the mountains, thus getting an accurate fix on the advance of the seasons. He also kept a secret time stick with notches on it. Months were counted by moons, days by sleeps; there were no other time divisions except years. The Speaker was the town crier. He stood on a house top and announced ceremonies, news, and crop information. The Kiva Priest was a kind of sacristan in charge of the temple. The War Chief took care of defense in the days when defense was needed.

It was the clan chiefs who really ran things. Little government was needed; the people were amiable and quiet. If anyone misbehaved, ostracism and ridicule were usually enough to set him again upon the paths of righteousness. Behind every clan chief there was an old woman who was

The Speaker

*Presentation
to the sun*

the real power in her clan, for these people traced descent through the mother, and the women owned the houses they built. Land was divided among the clans and held by them. In later days, when the United States Government parceled out the land of the Hopi to individuals, the recipients of the grants paid no attention to them whatever and clan ownership went on as before.

Children

Anyone born a Pueblo Indian faced a life of ceremony. It began on the evening of the child's nineteenth day, the days having been counted by scratches on the house wall. Guests brought gifts of corn meal, were given food to eat, and departed.

In the dark of the following morning the child's mother took a sweat bath for which juniper tea was substituted for water. After that her hair was ritually shampooed, and at dawn the guests returned. The baby was bathed and each guest rubbed soaproot suds on his head with an ear of corn. He was dusted with corn meal while his godmother prayed for a long life for him and offered the name she had chosen. Thereupon each guest presented an additional name. Any one of them might chance to stick. The many-named babe was then bound to his cradleboard for the first time. It was a light frame made of willow twigs and cushioned with frayed juniper bark.

The godmother now made a path of meal through the doorway, and at a signal from the father, who was outside, she carried the baby along her path to the edge of the mesa and presented him to the rising sun, casting a pinch of meal sunward as she did so. The baby's mother, wearing her wedding blanket, stood behind the godmother, and behind her, the guests lined up in silence. A feast followed and as each guest left he received a gift in return for the one he had given the night before.

As the baby grew up he learned by playing-at-working, and the whole population took a hand in his training. He learned his religion by watching ceremonies. He saw the sacred Kachinas, and he was given dolls dressed like them to play with. A child's success at games or craft was given unstinted applause by anyone who saw it. Children were seldom punished and were almost never struck. Punishment of very bad children was a duty of the Kachinas. A happy life; sometimes made happier when rain created beautiful mud puddles to be wallowed in.

Marriage

So long as he kept his eyes outside his own clan, a Pueblo youth was free to choose his own mate, or think he did. The announcement of an engagement was made by the girl combing the boy's hair in public. For three days before the wedding, the bride ground corn in her future mother-in-law's

Spinner

house to demonstrate her value as a wife. At the end of the ordeal her friends brought trays of meal as gifts—there couldn't be too much corn meal. The trays were returned next day with select ears of corn on them.

The girl's squash-blossom hairdress was loosened on her wedding day and her hair was shampooed by her mother-in-law, while her own mother was washing the groom's hair. The wedding guests arrived at dawn, each bringing water and using it to rinse the newly washed heads. The bride's hair was dressed in the squash-fruit hanks, as she would wear it the rest of her life, and the couple went together to the edge of the mesa to greet the rising sun in silence, touching their lips with meal and casting it to the sun. This was the marriage ceremony and they returned to the house for the wedding breakfast.

The couple lived a while with the husband's family; some essential matters had to be attended to before they could leave. The groom's father distributed raw cotton through the pueblo and his friends removed the seeds from it. Then he gave a feast in the kiva and all of the guests spun the cotton into yarn. At once, the groom and his male relatives set to weaving and produced two tasseled blankets, a white sash with fringe, and a mat in which they could be rolled for storage. A new pair of women's moccasins was also made. The bride put on this finery and went home to her mother's house, taking her husband with her.

Every January all the brides of the previous year turned out in their wedding clothes again for the ceremony that bade farewell to the Kachinas, who were going underground for a spell. After that the larger of the two blankets was used for whatever purpose a blanket might serve, but the smaller one was carefully kept. It was worn at the baptism of the first-born child and it served the woman one more time, as her shroud.

Death

Hopi burials were in the ground at the foot of the mesa. The body was sewn in a blanket and placed in a sitting position with a cotton mask over the face. For once there was little ceremony. Food was left by the grave and renewed for four days. The Pueblo people believed that their ancestors came from underground and that the "breath-

127

body" of the dead returned there along the path of the setting sun. The journey took four days. Souls were tested during this trip, and if they were *too* bad, they were destroyed. The dead were believed to retain a benevolent interest in the living and to return among them for a part of every year. Most of the Kachinas were representations of departed ancestors.

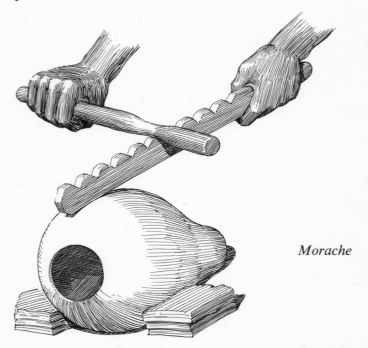

Morache

Music

The Hopi were the best musicians of all the Pueblos. Their religious chants were not beautiful, but their casual songs were appealing. They were song makers by nature and actually sold songs to other Indians. They had a bell-mouthed flute with five holes that produced shrill sounds. Most Indians used the flute only for courting but the Hopi had a flute ceremony.

They used gourd rattles to keep time, and dancers wore leg rattles made by stringing small bones so as to dangle across tortoise shells. They also had a curious instrument called by its Spanish name, *morache*. It was nothing more than a notched stick that could be rested on a dried gourd serving as a sound box and rubbed with a second stick, or a bone. It made the kind of noise one would expect such an instrument to make.

Tortoise-shell rattle

Gourd rattle

Religion

The Pueblo religion was far too ramified to be described in any detail here; it was the most elaborate one practiced by any Indians in North America. There was a different ceremony for every moon. Some were repeated once a year, some every two years, and others but once in four years. The Sun Priest had need of his notched stick to keep track of them. Bizarre costumes were used in all of the ceremonies and elaborate properties were made for them with much skill and labor. Nearly all of the rituals had the same purpose: to cajole rain from the gods. The famous Snake Ceremony had that object. Snakes were collected from the four cardinal points, the Four Winds. During nine days they were washed, prayed over, and purified in the kiva. Finally they were brought out to participate as brothers in a dance, at the end of which they were taken back to the desert and re-

leased, again to the Four Winds, as messengers to the gods imploring rain.

The center of the religion and the scene of many secret rituals was the kiva. It was a subterranean, or partially subterranean, chamber that could be entered only by a ladder through a hole in its roof. The roof was wood. Among the Hopi, the rest of the kiva was stone, with the walls plastered over with mud. At the foot of the ladder there was a fireplace and at another point in the floor there was a square hole that represented the entrance to the underworld from whence the people and the gods had come. After the sun, the principal deity was the Spider Woman, who was the sun's wife and who spun the rain clouds; below her in rank were all kinds and conditions of gods.

The Kachinas were benign spirits serving as intercessors. They were part of all ceremonies from July until January. Then they went back underground. They were enacted by men wear-

The climax of the Snake Ceremony.
Two Snake priests and an Antelope priest.

A Mudhead, a Koshare, *and one of the many* Kachinas

ing grotesque masks and special costumes, and no one pretended otherwise; but everyone, including the actors, was able to accept the presence of the actual spirits. In spite of their weird visages, there was something charming about the Kachinas.

The ritual imagination of the Pueblos was by no means exhausted by the Kachinas. Clowns, called Koshare, were provided to lighten the solemnity of the ceremonials. They were painted all over in broad white-and-black stripes to symbolize skeletons, and they were not required to respect any person or any thing. There were other clowns, too, known as *goyemshi,* or Mudheads. They represented the men who first emerged from a hole in the earth.

Prayer sticks were provided for ordinary day-to-day piety; little paddles painted with symbols and decked out in feathers that could be left in a cornfield, by a spring, or wherever it was felt that a prayer was needed.

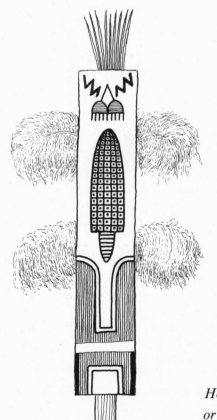

Hopi baho,
or prayer stick

129

A Shuswap winter house somewhat dismembered to show its construction. The scaffold is for storage of food.

10

The Northerners

Indians weren't aware of a dividing line between the United States and Canada; parts of some tribes we have already met lived north of the Great Lakes. There were more Blackfeet, more Assinaboine, and more Chippewa north of the lakes than south of them. The Neutrals lived mostly in Canada north of Lake Ontario. They and the Hurons were of Iroquois blood but they never stopped fighting their New York cousins until those cousins had all but obliterated them.

The rest of eastern Canada was Algonquian except perhaps for the Beothuk of Newfoundland, who seem to have been unique but who were wiped out so early that nobody knows much about them. They habitually wore a coat of red ocher on their skins. One may guess that John Cabot's encounter with them in 1497 may have had something to do with tagging all Indians as "red men."

The plateau between the Coast Range and the

Rocky Mountains extends far into Canada; today, the Alcan Highway traverses it. On it, just over the international boundary, the main body of the Kutenai paddled their ram-bowed canoes and spoke a language they seem to have shared with no one. Here, too, was the heartland of the Salishan tribes who had buffalo-hunting cousins in Montana and fishing cousins scattered along the Pacific coast. The Shuswap were a typical tribe of the Interior Salish. They dressed like woodland Indians and built bark canoes, sometimes copying those of the Kutenai. They traded with the coastal Indians and borrowed ideas of social rank from them; as a result, they divided themselves into nobles and commoners—about half and half—and slaves, mostly obtained in trade.

In summer the Shuswap lived in bark-covered lodges that were barely rainproof, but in winter they moved into dwellings that weren't dupli-

130

cated anywhere on the continent. These houses were cone-shaped with a smoke-hole entrance at the apex. They were solidly constructed of logs over a circular pit about four feet deep. The excavated earth was used to cover the roof. A notched log, standing in the smoke hole, served as a staircase; everybody who used it shattered dirt on the occupants below.

North of the Shuswap a string of Athapascan tribes, cut off by the Rockies from the main body of their people, occupied the narrowing plateau all the way to its northern end. Perhaps the most interesting of these are the Carrier, so called from their gruesome custom of forcing widows to carry the charred scraps of their late husbands' bones in baskets on their backs for three years.

The Carrier were in close touch with the more advanced coastal people, and like the Shuswap they took over ideas of social prestige from them. From the same source they took the idea of celebrating an important event with a feast at which all the guests received presents that they were expected to even up when they gave a feast. The Carrier people also shared a curious custom with some other Athapascans: when parents named their first-born son, they dropped their own names entirely and were known henceforth as the parents of so-and-so.

These Indians and their neighbors to the north hunted and were especially good trappers but they depended for food mainly on salmon. Their land was one of many rivers, and the spawning fish teemed clear up to the headwaters. The Carrier followed an unvarying yearly schedule: hunting large animals in the early winter; salmon fishing in the spring; moving to the mountains in midsummer to trap marmots; and trekking down to the coast in the fall to trade. From midwinter

until spring they holed up and lived on their accumulated supplies.

The Caribou Hunters

East of the mountains, all the way across to Hudson's Bay and northward far into the barren tundra, were more Athapascans. In their own language they called themselves *Tinneh* (Dené) which, as usual, means The People. They were divided by differing dialects and customs into tribes but they had no real tribal organization. Each small band kept to itself.

The Dené were all nomad hunters who sometimes did a little fishing on the side. There were Athapascans in south-central Canada, the Sarcee, who had nearly every attribute of Plains Indians. But buffalo didn't range very far north, so most of the Dené hunted caribou; sometimes on snowshoes in the woods and sometimes following the herds in their summer migration northward, with a wary eye on the horizon for hostile Eskimo who were looking for the same animals.

Summer hunting on the tundra involved a whole band driving the caribou into prepared enclosures for slaughter. They also took many by spearing them from canoes as the herds were swimming rivers and lakes. So long as these methods were used the caribou population held its own, but with guns the Indians could kill too many; and they have nearly shot themselves out of a living.

The Dené didn't depend entirely on one kind of animal; there were some moose (though they are said to be more plentiful now than formerly), bear, deer, and smaller game. Big lake trout abounded.

Etchaottine spearing caribou

Kutchin in summer

The People

The Athapascans were sturdy but as a rule they didn't live to great age. Their faces clearly showed their Mongoloid origin. The nose was fairly straight and not large; the eyes had a definite slant; the cheek bones were high and prominent but not so heavy as those of Indians further south.

Dené hair was as straight, as black, and as coarse as any Indian hair.

There was a female-line clan system carried so far that a father wasn't considered related to his children. Hence if a man wished to marry his father's niece or even his father's sister, no one saw any objection to his doing so.

The bands had chiefs but they held only as much authority as they were strong enough to grasp and they might at any time have to give place to a stronger man. It was the shaman who really ran things. Why wouldn't he? He was thought to have complete control of the weather and to be capable of all but dictating a hunter's luck. Further, he could either cure or kill with magic. He could be hired to perform either of these functions, and though he might get into trouble if he couldn't explain a cure gone wrong, no punishment was dealt him for murder. The victim's family vented their wrath on the man who had hired the shaman.

The Dené have been studied less thoroughly than any large group of Indians and they are now so changed by white contact that further study is difficult. That they didn't all hold the same ideas is known. For instance, they tended to murder or abandon the aged and infirm, but there was a group, the Etchaottine (Slaves), who were kind to old people, even though their presence made a difficult life even harder.

There were a couple of tribes in which women were well treated, but for the most part a woman's

Chipewyan lodge

lot was so hard that mothers often killed girl babies as an act of mercy. The Kutchin women were abject slaves. They hauled sleds, built lodges, and carried burdens. The men didn't even bring home the game they killed; they sent the women after it. Curiously, however, the Kutchin men did the cooking, and the women ate what the men left.

Polygamy was generally practiced. When a man's eye was caught by a likely looking woman he challenged her husband to a wrestling match, and if he won, the woman was his. Strong men had the greatest number of wives. Since they also acquired the greatest number of hides and needed porters for them, this worked out very well.

Ideas absorbed from people on the Dené borders were passed far into the hinterlands. They learned to make canoes from the Algonquians and made excellent ones, using birch bark as far west and north as it could be had and spruce or cedar beyond the range of birch. Between fights, they traded with the Eskimo and learned from them to tailor hides into well-fitting shirts with long tails fore and aft and legging-pants with moccasins attached. In cold weather two shirts were worn: one hair-side in, next to the skin, with another, hair-side out, over it. Such garments were made and worn by Athapascans who lived too far south ever to see an Eskimo. There was no great difference between the clothes of men and those of women: trousers; hooded shirts somewhat longer than the men's, fitted loosely to the body and made with sleeves; and fur mittens that hung from a cord passing through the sleeves. Babies were kept in fur-lined bags or in bark cradles.

These nomads needed a portable dwelling and what they used was a skin-covered tepee. It was smaller and much lower in proportion to its width than the tepee of the Plains and it had no smoke flaps. When they holed up for the winter, the Kutchin built domed wigwams. These were cov-

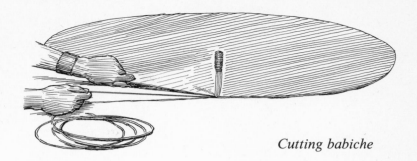

Cutting babiche

ered with skins and piled with snow. The floors were spread thickly with fir boughs.

The Athapascans gave back some things for what they took. They invented porcupine quillwork and did some of the best of it. It's possible that the sinew-backed bow was introduced by them; perhaps brought in from Asia long ago. The tribes called Yellow Knives earned their name by mining copper and selling it southward and westward. The Dené made beautiful snowshoes and perhaps the northern Algonquians learned the art from them.

Babiche

The cutting of babiche, the leather string that netted snowshoes and was used constantly wherever string was needed, certainly originated with the Dené and so, as noted earlier, did the toboggan. The far northern Indians had to use babiche as string because they usually lacked the vegetable substitutes that more southerly people had. Babiche was cut spirally, as a continuous strip, by pulling a hide against a fixed blade. It could be made very narrow at need, and the Indians were skillful at keeping the width of it constant. The hide used was merely scraped, not tanned in any way. Babiche cut from deer- or moosehide and used wet shrank as it dried and thus made an extremely tight lashing. It is said that babiche

Moving

made from caribou hide would neither stretch nor shrink, which made it the best to use for snowshoes.

Toboggans

Temporary toboggans could be made of birch bark but they weren't very durable; most toboggans were spruce. They were made of two boards split out with wedges from a log and shaved down with a crooked knife to half an inch or less in thickness. Toboggans came in many sizes; the largest, described here, required boards thirteen feet long. One edge of each board was made straight and smooth, so the two could lie close together. Even in country where trees were large enough to provide a single board for a toboggan, two were preferred; they were less likely to split and two gave resilience to the sled in rough going.

The outer edges of the boards were tapered toward both ends, leaving a five-foot section in the middle of the toboggan that was about eighteen inches wide. The front end was about half that wide and the back was still narrower, seven inches or less. No guess can be given on the reason for the taper; it would seem to waste cargo space and to create some tendency for the sled to plow into the snow.

The boards were held together by five or six transverse battens lashed to their upper sides with rawhide. The lashings passed through holes in the boards and lay in grooves on the underside, so as to get no wear in travel. Each batten had four lashings, securing each board in two places.

A couple of feet of the front end of the toboggan was boiled until it became soft and flexible. The front batten was then attached to the extreme end, and the softened part was rolled up and back; finished, it stood about a foot and a half high. Permanent guys, stretched from the first batten down to the second, kept the prow from straightening out again. Rawhide lines, lying on the deck, were run along both sides of the toboggan. The battens were grooved to allow these lines to pass under them. Cargo lashings were made fast to the lines. Two twenty-five foot traces were used to pull the sled, with extra shorter ones for the dogs, if they helped. The principal reason for fastening dogs to a toboggan was to keep them from running off; they weren't huskies.

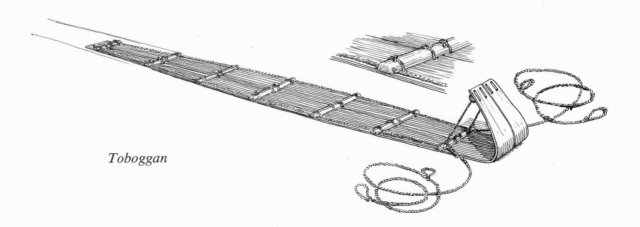

Toboggan

One end of a Haida town

11

The Coast Townsmen

On the western coast of North America the mountains face the sea, and along the northern half of it they come so close to the water that only a strip of habitable shore is left. Rivers have made deep fiords through the mountain chain. The Japan Current passes this coast, and when the warmed air over it hits the cold slopes, rain falls; but the shore is never very cold in winter. That's why the earliest immigrants came this way.

Centuries later other people moved in because they could get a living out of the sea. It was a bountiful living; it allowed the leisure necessary to develop art, elaborate ceremonials, and a strictly ordered social system. Indians who attained these things usually did so on the fruits of agriculture. Here, nothing was grown except a little tobacco; the sea was enough. Its bounty also

fostered a situation that occurred nowhere else on the continent: a dense population in a strictly limited space. This forced competition and the claiming of choice townsites and fishing rights. The recurring result was war, real war this time, that exterminated the vanquished or enslaved them.

Indians With Whiskers

The occupied strip extended from the point on the Alaskan coast where it turns definitely southward down to the mouth of the Columbia River. Throughout its length people had similar ideas and did things in ways so nearly alike that they may be considered as a unit. They weren't all the same kind of people, however. In the north

the Tlingit and the Haida were related to the Dené, though undoubtedly they also had other blood. The Tsimshian spoke a language with but two near relatives; and the Kwakiutl and Nootka languages were similar to one another but unlike any other known tongue. In addition to these there were smaller groups speaking a babel of dialects derived from the Salishan language of the northern plateau. Most of these Salishans were in what is now the State of Washington. They were influenced by the ideas of their northern neighbors but they didn't accept all of them.

Naturally people with so many different origins didn't all look alike. Those of the north had quite light skins and sometimes brown or even reddish hair. The men often wore mustaches and beards. Some of the southerners had quite dark skins, and looking at old photographs of them, it's possible to see something in the claim that has been made for a Polynesian connection. It seems certain that racial strains were mixed in here that weren't in other Indians. The majority of the men were stockily built, with the heavy chests and strong shoulders that result from constant paddling.

The Tlingit and the Haida followed their relatives of the interior in the matter of clans and inheritance through the female line. Farther south inheritance was the other way. In either case, inheritance was a matter of far greater importance to these people than it was to other Indians.

Regardless of the language they spoke or the large groups in which we may classify them, the coast Indians weren't organized as tribes. Their unit was the town, which might or might not be loosely federated with other towns. A town was a row of houses in a fiord or along the shore in the lee of an island where several hundred people lived, thirty or forty to a house. Two or more clans shared a town, or the inhabitants were divided arbitrarily into halves, like drawing up sides. In either case, marriage had to be outside one's own section. Each house belonged to a large family and had its own chief. One house chief was also the town chief, a position of prestige and wealth that was hereditary.

Dwellings

Houses north of Puget Sound had gable roofs. Those of the Tlingit and the Haida were generally similar, but those of the Haida were the better. The coast people were fine woodworkers—far ahead of any other Indians—and the Haida were the best of the coast people. Haida houses were of enormously heavy construction and the largest of them might be forty feet wide by one hundred and twenty feet long. They were rectangular, with four corner posts projecting somewhat above the level of the eaves and two end posts that supported the ridge beam. Additional posts stiffened the side walls. The front ridge-pole post rose some ten or twelve feet above the roof and was carved all over with heraldic crests and with records of history, real or fabulous. The carving was painted. The door of a Haida house was an opening in this post included in the carved design as part of an heraldic animal. The two front corner posts were also carved and were credited with supernatural powers, such as warning the occupants of approaching danger. Houses of almost identical form were built by the Maori in New Zealand.

The big beams that the posts supported were carefully squared and skillfully joined. The sills between the bottoms of the posts were deeply grooved along their upper surfaces to receive the butts of wide planks that made the walls. The plates connecting the posts at the top of the walls were similarly rabbeted on their lower surfaces. The wall planks stood vertical and had to be put into place as the frame was built, instead of being added to the finished frame. Except for the labor of splitting them from the log and hewing them smooth with primitive tools, boards four or five feet wide presented no problem, since the heavy rainfall caused evergreen trees to attain really impressive size.

The pitch of the roof was quite flat. A smoke hole was left open at the ridge. What little daylight reached the inside came through this and the door. There were no windows.

A large rectangular pit, about knee-deep, was dug in the middle of the interior. It was floored with wood, as was the wide ground-level platform that surrounded it. On this platform, against the back wall and, if necessary, the side walls, each subunit of the family built itself a cubicle, often a simplified replica of the large house, roof and all. In the pit, near a center post that helped to support the ridge, a single fireplace served all the occupants.

South of the Haida, the Kwakiutl and the Nootka built much cruder-looking houses of similar shape and size, though with much flatter roofs. These people were in the habit of moving their towns, according to the season, from one fishing site to another. At each site they had permanent house frames set up. When they moved, they dis-

mantled the walls and roof and took the planking with them, lashed across two canoes. The house frames were as heavy as those of the Haida but they were concealed by the walls. Small posts were set close to the outside of the main frame, and the wall planks were slid in behind them horizontally and tied in place. The door was a simple opening in the front wall.

Such a house had a dirt floor and the cousins and nephews were allotted family spaces along the side walls, with an eight-foot aisle left down the middle. There were no partitions. Each family had its own fire and pushed a roof plank aside with a pole to let the smoke out. The Nootka carved faces on their house posts. They showed inside the building and had no known meaning; they were purely decorations.

Family crests were usually painted on the outside of the front wall, and a carved representation of one of them capped a tall pole that stood near the entrance. This was the simplest form of the so-called totem pole; so-called, because this crest was not a clan totem. Even in the north, where everybody belonged to a clan and each clan had its totem animal, that animal wasn't represented on

Kwakiutl house

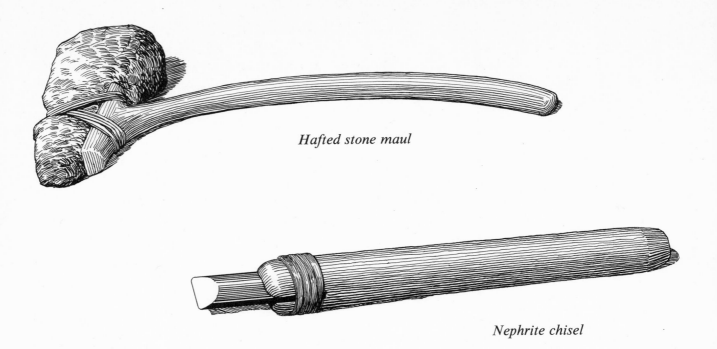

Hafted stone maul

Nephrite chisel

the carved totem poles. Those poles developed from the house posts of the Haida and they were displays of the pretensions of an individual chief. Totem poles reached their highest development after the Indians obtained steel tools.

Totem poles were often put up by the chief's heir as a memorial reciting the deceased's ancestry and deeds, and also as a proclamation of the heir's right to his honors. Quite often a totem pole was a tomb as well as a monument. The dead chief was interred in a cavity hollowed in the column or was placed in a box on the top of it.

Woodwork

The stone of the coast was largely volcanic and difficult to work, so except for a few articles, the Indians let it alone and concentrated their efforts on wood. Most of the trees, but not all, were evergreens: cedar, redwood, spruce, hemlock, yew. The warmth of the sea encouraged some deciduous trees, such as oak and alder, along the shore. The Tlingit in the north had little but hemlock, so they imported better wood by trading. Trees were felled with chisels made of elkhorn or of nephrite, which is inferior jade. These were hafted and were driven into the wood with stone mauls. Most of

the mauls were hand hammers but some had hafts. The labor of felling trees six or seven feet thick was considerable.

Once a tree was down it could be split into planks with maul-driven wedges of yew wood, which is tough and close-grained. The tops of the wedges were tightly served with spruce root to help them resist the blows of the mauls. Red cedar and redwood were best for planks because they split easily. Haida house planks were more than an inch thick and the thickness of them had to

Stone mauls
(the smaller is about ten inches high)

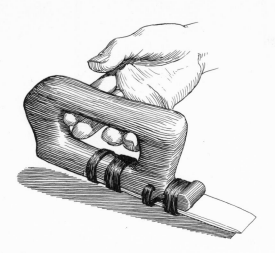

Hand adz with a bone blade

Boxes and Woodenware

Much use was made of planks only half an inch thick for making boxes, which served the same purposes to which other Indians put mocucks, pottery, parfleches, and baskets. The coast dwellers made no pottery and had no birch bark, and though they made good baskets, the climate was too damp to allow using them for storage. Wooden boxes served as storage cases and also as pots for stone boiling; as drums; as buckets; as quivers; as cradles; and as coffins. Storage boxes and cooking boxes were nearly cubical, though the Nootka made tall ones. Coffins were proportioned for a body in a flexed position. Quivers were appropriately shaped; so were tackle boxes, which were angled to fit into the narrow ends of canoes. The work on all of them was done with skill that approaches modern cabinetmaking. Almost any of them would hold water.

The cradle used by these Indians seems more normal to a white man than do most Indian cradles. The long narrow box had a head higher than its sides or foot. There were no rockers on it but it could be suspended in a horizontal position from a branch and easily bounced or swung. The baby was swaddled and tied in.

A split plank for a box was dressed smooth on both sides. It was as wide as the height of the box and as long as all four sides, since they were made as one piece. To accomplish this, deep grooves were cut across the plank where three of the corners would be. The wood was then steamed and folded with the kerfs on the inside. The ends were fastened together, where they met at the fourth corner, either by pegging or by lashing. Curiously, these ingenious people didn't know about the bow

be controlled exactly so they would fit the grooves prepared for them.

The most used tool of these people was a bone adz. It has been given its name by white men. While it was used somewhat as a hand adz is, it was also a chisel and a plane. The user pulled the blade toward him. It's difficult to imagine how a sliver of bone could be given a real cutting edge but apparently it could. Most adzes had D-shaped wooden handles, like the one illustrated, but there were several other shapes. Iron knives were never common but these Indians had them long before they met Europeans. It's been suggested that the metal came from wrecked ships but it seems more probable that the Indians got it by trade from Siberia, where there were tribes that mined and worked iron.

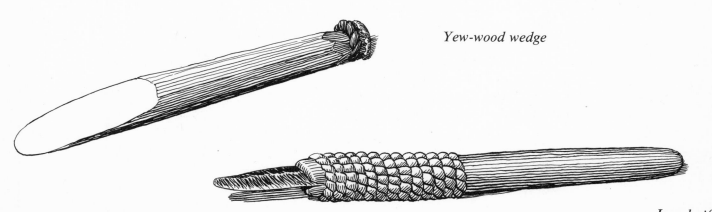

Yew-wood wedge

Iron knife

Kwakiutl cradle.
The baby wears a pressure board to deform his head.
His mother is shredding cedar bark for weaving.

the bottoms. They were not pegged of course. Tlingit and Haida lids were themselves shallow boxes that slipped on over the main box, much as we lid a shoe box.

A storage box was netted with permanent tie ropes of cedar bark ending in four loops that could be slipped over the corners of the lid. Lashing these loops together secured the cover. Boxes were often decorated handsomely, either by painting or by carving in low relief. The ornament was applied to the front and sides; the lid and the back were plain.

Boat-shaped dishes and round-bowled dippers were shaped from alder or soft yellow cedar. Food dishes (they were really troughs) for feasts were three or four feet long and held about fifteen gallons of fish stew. They sometimes represented conventionalized animals or had such animals carved at their ends. These people were able to carve very realistically but they usually preferred not to do so.

Canoes

Though there were two main shapes and many sizes of canoes used on the coast, the methods for making all of them were similar. The largest boats were over sixty feet long and as much as eight feet wide. They were all dugouts made of white cedar. This wood splits easily and this was bad for canoes; one major split and the work of weeks was ruined. To avoid it the hull was excavated a little

drill. They used a piece of bone as a bit, stuck it into the end of a stick, and spun the stick between their palms.

The plank used for the bottom of a box was thicker than that for the sides and was rabbeted on all four edges, as was the bottom edge of the box. The two fitted each other precisely and were pegged into place from the bottom. Storage boxes had lids. Those of the Kwakiutl and the Nootka often had a convex bulge and were rabbeted like

The parts of a Nootka storage box
ready to be put together

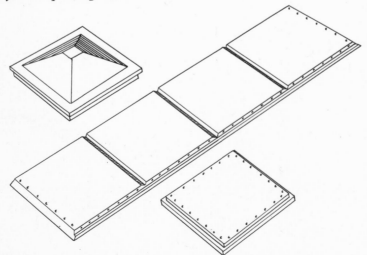

Painted storage box

Small wooden food dish

at a time. Fire was not used. The chisel and maul did the rough work, and the adz was used for finishing. The outside was shaped with the same tools. A canoe was usually started in the fall and completed by two men in six months.

When the log had been shaped and emptied, the hull was filled with water which was heated with hot stones to soften the wood. This allowed the sides of the canoe to be spread and stout thwarts were forced in to keep them so. The thwarts of a large canoe were about four feet apart.

All Haida canoes had high ends to make them more seaworthy. It wasn't possible to form these from the main log, so they were shaped from separate pieces, fitted on with precise scarf joints, and secured by lashing and pegging. So far were the added pieces carried back into the hull that an appearance of considerable sheer, or curve upward toward the ends, was produced. The outsides

of the canoes were blackened by charring and oiling. The hulls of war boats were often decorated in yellow, black, and white, and some had crest animals carved at their bows.

Haida canoes were either purchased or copied along most of the coast. Even the Kwakiutl, pretty far to the south, used the Haida shape. The cutwater of a Haida canoe was almost vertical. Above it a prow, like the head of a medieval ship, projected far over the water. The stern rose in an easy curve from a counter, rounded to deal with following seas. Though its bottom was round, this was a good boat for deep-sea fishing, with some of the merits of a New England dory. When the seas were too high or the catch too heavy, inflated sealskins were tied along the gunwales to act as sponsons.

The Nootka needed a boat of different shape for their pursuit of whales. It, too, had added ends but they were lower than those of a Haida boat. The stern was vertical. The bow was almost exactly the shape of the bow of a clipper ship. A strip of the bottom was completely flat, the sides angling out from it at about forty-five degrees at the waist.

The paddles used in the Northwest had a shape of their own. A T-shaped crutch top was carved on the handle, and the blade was pointed at the bottom. The Nootka sometimes added a six-inch spur to the bottom of their paddle so that water

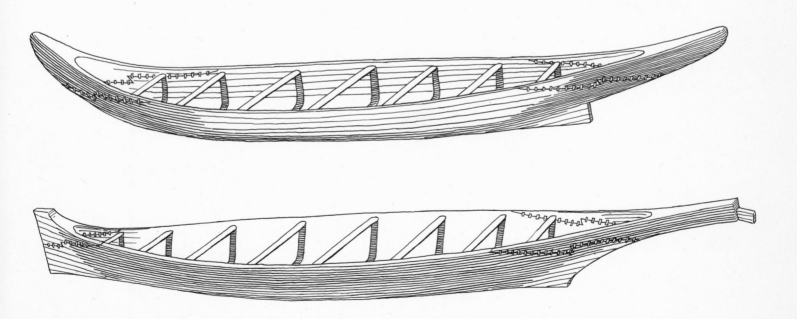

Comparison of the shapes of Haida (top) and Nootka canoes.
The bows are on the right.

Canoe paddle

would drip from it quietly and not disturb a dozing whale.

It's certain that the Northwesterners used bark fiber sails on their canoes at an early date. They sailed only before the wind. Some think they caught the idea from European ships but others have suggested that their ancestors brought sailing with them. Then, too, the Chinese have been expert sailors for centuries; it would be strange if no ancient junk ever followed the Japan Current and coasted along here, demonstrating her sails as she went.

Silhouettes for comparison

Kwakiutl war dugout, before 1850

Maori war dugout, from an old New Zealand rock carving

Some war canoes once were built with high shields on their bows, loopholed for bowmen assaulting a beach. White men saw them and drew them before they disappeared. Comparison of the silhouette of an old Nootka war canoe from one of these drawings with the profile of a war canoe from an ancient New Zealand rock carving is suggestive.

Fishing

Salmon go up rivers to spawn, and once they have done so, they die. The Indians, seeing this but not understanding it, believed the fish were sacrificing themselves to feed men. This idea was enlarged to include the reincarnation of the salmon in the sea. All a salmon needed to live again and repeat his sacrifice was his backbone; so the scraps of meals were religiously returned to the water.

It wasn't necessary to wait for the salmon to die naturally. They were caught in traps or speared. Spearing a fish in clear water presents a difficulty; due to the refraction of light, the fish isn't actually where he appears to be. There's compensation to a miss, however. A wooden spear thrown into deep water will return butt-first to the hand of the thrower, so long as it strikes nothing and isn't swept away by current.

Spears were made so that the heads came off the shafts once the quarry was struck, but the point was still connected with the shaft by a short piece of line. This gave a thirty-pound salmon with high horsepower a chance to thrash around without breaking the spear shaft. Tlingit spearheads were carved from one piece of bone but those of the Kwakiutl and other southern tribes were ingeniously barbed by assembling several parts. For deep water two of them were mounted on a slender forked shaft fifteen feet long. Single spearheads for exceptionally large fish were attached to a hand line and came entirely clear of the shaft when they struck. After the fish was struck, inflated bladders were tied to the line as close to the catch as possible, to help in tiring him.

One kind of salmon trap was made by sinking a bulging cylindrical "basket" in a narrow opening in a fence built across a stream. The basket was

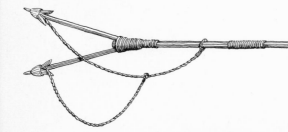

Salmon spear

Salmon trap.
The weir is omitted
on one side for clarity.

made of slender poles and could be five feet in diameter and twenty feet long. Its upstream end was closed and a much shorter basketry funnel was inserted into its open end, with the point of the cone upstream. The large end of the funnel was also open and its rim fitted into the rim of the big basket. The small end of the funnel was just large enough to allow a salmon to pass through it. Driven by a primordial urge to get upstream, a fish wouldn't readily seek a downstream exit. Trapped fish were speared through an opening in the top of the trap.

All of these Indians fished at sea with hand lines, and here too, there were local variations in the equipment. Toward the south, hooks for large fish were made of springy spruce, steamed to shape and equipped with bone points. The northerners used a much heavier hook made of hardwood and carved with the owner's crest for luck. This kind, too, had a bone point. The stems of kelp were used as fishing lines. This seaweed grows in deep water and reaches the surface; so its slender stems are very long and they are very tough. The Indians soaked the stems in fresh

water, oiled them, and dried them. Two hooks with a sinker between them were often hung from a straight spreader.

Salmon were hooked near the mouths of rivers, and halibut and cod were caught in the sea. Some of them were so large that it was necessary to kill them with a club before they could be boated. Cod weighing two hundred pounds were caught in these waters. A 19th-century writer says the Nootka enticed them to the surface with bait and then speared them. Other Indians must have used different methods, however, because two kinds of cod hooks are known.

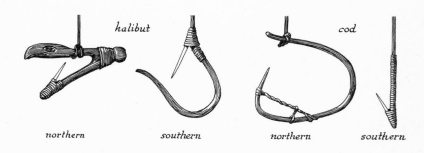

Fishhooks of wood and bone

143

Many kinds of smaller fish were taken in their seasons and on special fishing grounds. Among them was the eulachon, so thoroughly saturated with oil that the dried body of one of them could be burned like a candle. It was its oiliness that made this fish popular as food; these Indians loved the flavor of fish oil!

Head of a Nootka whale harpoon

Whaling

A whale was a bonanza as a source of oil, meat, bone, and sinew. Any of the coast people were glad to find a dead one—even an overripe one was better than no whale—but only the Nootka went to sea and killed whales. A whole flotilla of canoes, carrying ten men each, hunted the whale. They were all under the command of a chief who "owned" the whale and inherited his right to strike with the first harpoon. The crews purified themselves for three months before the hunt. They were strictly disciplined and minutely trained; and the spirits of departed harpooners were duly propitiated to give them help. When they found a whale idling on the surface, the squadron hung back while the chief's boat approached the animal silently from behind. The harpooner stood on the gunwale near the bow balancing the heavy ten-foot shaft of his weapon athwartship.

The head of the harpoon was made in three pieces: a keen-edged point shaped from a giant mussel shell and two elkhorn barbs. The three parts were stuck together with pine gum and tightly lashed with whale sinew. The head came wholly off its shaft after the whale was struck. One end of a nine-foot leader of whale sinew was made fast to the head and was caught to the shaft with easily broken thongs. The leader's other end was bent to a three-hundred-foot line, which was coiled in the boat as carefully as ever a New England whaler coiled his. There was a difference though; the end of the Yankee line was made fast to the whaleboat—the Nootka line was free to go overboard. It had inflated sealskin drags on it at intervals. The line itself was cedar-bark fiber and was stronger for its thickness than a hemp rope.

The harpoon was too heavy to throw. When the canoe was within a couple of feet of the whale, the chief thrust with all the power he could muster and dropped into the bottom of the boat as the yelling paddlers bent to sheering away, so as not to be swamped by the whale's tail. A fool-hardy chief would sometimes gain glory, perhaps posthumous, by jumping from the boat onto the whale's back. The leader of the second canoe had the honor of putting the next harpoon into the whale. After that it was anyone's turn and more and more harpoons were added, each with its string of floats. The whale might eventually have forty or fifty inflated skins hanging on him.

Nootka whaling

His actions were thus much inhibited and it was possible to follow him until he had exhausted himself. Then the hunters rendered him completely helpless by severing the tendons of his tail with a spade-shaped lance, and a spear with a long slender point was thrust into his heart to finish him. Holes were made in the whale's lips, and his mouth was tied shut so that he couldn't fill with water and sink. Then the whole squadron put lines on him and set out to tow him home. If the gods were good, the whale had run toward shore; if not, it might take a couple of days of laborious paddling to get him where he was wanted.

Hunting

In addition to fish and whales, there were porpoises in the sea; and seals and sea otters to be hunted for their flesh and their pelts. The fur of the sea otter is very handsome. It was used by chiefs for their robes, and since the animals were never plentiful, a sea-otter pelt was one of the possessions by which wealth was reckoned. The otter was by nature unsuspicious of man and once found it was readily shot with arrows from canoes. Seals were hunted with harpoons and inflated drags, much as whales were. They had to be killed with clubs before they could be boated.

Hunting on land was everywhere secondary to fishing. Most of it was done by the people of towns well up the steep-banked rivers, and the greater part of the game was taken with deadfalls and snares. Deerhides were valued but elkhide, thicker and tougher, was more highly esteemed. The

Nootka wore overlapping bandages of it from hips to armpits as armor in war. Bears were also taken for their meat and fur. These Indians would eat the meat of land animals only if it were very fresh, a reversal of their attitude toward fish, which was relished in a state that would make a white man run from it.

The most arduous hunting was for mountain goats, wanted for their wool from which blankets were woven and for their horns that were steamed and shaped into dippers. These animals are at least as agile as any known goat and they prefer to live on inaccessible crags. Hunting parties climbed above the goats and drove them downhill into narrow gorges that had been closed at one end. Dogs are said to have been trained to help with the driving. Once trapped, the goats were shot with arrows.

War and Weapons

Advanced though these northern people were in some ways, their ferocity in war and their wanton disregard of the life of an enemy or a slave mark them as perhaps more truly savages than any other Indians. It was their custom to start wars as unexpectedly as possible, landing their canoes at a village just before dawn and attempting to slaughter its inhabitants before they could arm themselves. Scalps didn't interest them; they took heads and mounted them on their canoes for a triumphant homecoming.

The attacks were often repulsed with bloody fighting, and when the invaders retreated, the

heads of their fallen warriors were set on poles in front of the defenders' houses. Not all of the wars were for the purpose of obtaining choice fishing grounds. Some were raids to capture accumulated wealth; some to avenge a murder; some to kill a proper number of people to accompany a chief on his death journey; still others were slave raids. Anyone captured could be enslaved and could usually be ransomed, but early writings indicate a slave class also: a class considered to have been born inferior.

The Tlingit used armor in war. Wooden rods set side by side and held together with twine made a cuirass that covered the whole torso, front and back. With luck, it might turn an arrow or a spear thrust. Greaves of similar construction protected the lower leg. A wide wooden collar resting on the warrior's shoulders supported a helmet of wood carved as a grotesque human head.

Short spears headed with copper or with the sharp tail of a sting ray were well adapted to canoe fighting, and there was a curious dagger of iron or whalebone that had a long blade below its hilt and a short one above it. Bows on the coast were

Tlingit armored for battle.
The collar and the helmet are separate units.

Tlingit double-pointed
dagger of bone.
There were iron ones
of the same shape.

Haida dagger
of native-mined copper

rather short and wide, with their ends turned back sharply toward the string. They were held horizontally to shoot arrows that had foreshafts equipped with bone points or points of shell. Slings were used, too, for throwing stones at enemy canoes. In fights between canoes the sharp-pointed paddles became effective weapons. The pick-like club known as a "slave killer" wasn't a war weapon. It was used for the public murder of slaves. This was committed casually to demonstrate that the chief who owned the slave and killed him or her was wealthy enough to be nonchalant about valuable property.

Clothing

In anything remotely resembling warm weather, clothes were conspicuous by their absence along the whole coast. The women contented themselves with a short apron and the men with a straightforward nothing. The breechclout was not worn. Everybody went barefoot most of the year, even in snow, though all of these people knew how to make moccasins. John Jewett, who was a prisoner of the Nootka from 1803 to 1805, says they went swimming every day of the year. Around

146

Nootka noble and two commoners.
They are dressed for a feast.

Vancouver Island the people wore tunics of cedar-bark cloth when they dressed up. Women wore these as straight sheaths, gathered at the neck and with armholes cut in them. The men hung them over one shoulder, leaving both arms free. Both sexes belted them at the waist. Robes were often worn over the tunics.

Up north more complete clothing was needed. The Tlingit learned tailoring from the Eskimos and passed the craft southward to their neighbors the Haida and the Tsimshian. As with the Dené, this knowledge produced leather pants and moccasins made as one garment, like a small child's night clothes, and fringed shirts of the same material made with true sleeves. Robes might be worn over them, like a cape.

Since rain was an ever-present problem in the area, special garments were needed for protection

against it. Round capes or square ponchos of cedar-bark cloth or of matting were worn with decorated basketry hats. The Nootka and their neighbors wore hats shaped like a squat straw beehive. Canoes and whales were painted on them in black and those worn by chiefs were topped with pointed knobs. The Haida wore a flatter hat with just a suggestion of a crown merging into a turned-down brim. These were painted with crest animals in the curious and fascinating way that the Haida seem to have originated. They felt it necessary to show all sides of an animal in one drawing and they did so by splitting him down the middle and flattening him out! They so conventionalized their drawings that the subject was identifiable only by a single carefully retained feature.

Some fiber from nettles was used wherever they

147

grew along the shore, but the principal source of yarn and twine was cedar bark. The bark was soaked two weeks in fresh water and beaten with clubs to remove the woody parts. The fiber was then shredded against the edge of a plank with a wooden blade. The resulting yarn was coarse. It was bleached and dyed. Its strands were long and it had great tensile strength. It was twisted by rolling against the leg, as the Algonquians rolled basswood. Weaving was done by the same twining method that was used by nearly all Indians: a half twist of two wefts between each pair of warps.

The Chilkat used cedar bark for the warp of their beautiful blankets that were copied and worn by all their northern neighbors. The weft was pre-dyed mountain-goat hair; blue, black, yellow, and white. The women wove these blankets varying them a little from the designs that the men painted for them on boards. All spaces were filled; these northerners abhorred an empty space. The warp hung loose from a bar. The elements of the design were woven as separate units and joined later. The ends of sections of warp

Haida decorated hat

that were not being worked were stowed in small bags. The finished blanket was shaped like a very wide shield. It had a deep fringe and was worn as a priest wears a cope. The chilkat blanket wasn't an everyday garment; it was intended for formal appearances only.

Tunics, aprons, and knee-length leggings patterned and woven in the same way were used for ceremonial dances. Like the blankets, they were worn with wooden headdresses carved with representations of the heads of animals or people and set off with crowns of sea-lion whiskers. A drapery of buckskin and ermine pelts hung to the wearer's shoulders on each side and to his hips in back.

Among the Nootka and Kwakiutl both sexes wore their hair long, except when it was cut as a sign of mourning. The men were likely to roll theirs up on their heads to keep it out of the way. Everyone greased his hair thoroughly, and when visiting or receiving guests he ornamented it by sticking bits of white down to it with pine gum. Northern men seem to have worn their hair short. Faces were painted all over for everyday weather protection and were decorated with painted crest animals or checkerboard squares for ceremonies. Tattooing of women was quite general, ranging from the simple chin stripes of Puget Sound to the repeated crests of the Haida that took up most of the space below the neck.

Tsimshian chief in headdress and chilkat blanket

148

When strange canoes appeared in the distance, all of the residents of a Nootka town rushed indoors and arrayed themselves with robes and paint and duck down and nose ornaments. Nearly everyone had his ears and the septum of his nose pierced. Rare spiral shells were the preferred nose decoration, but poor men had to be content with polished wooden rods that stuck out some eight inches on each side. The hole in the septum became so large that it wasn't unusual for a man who needed his hands free to thrust his pipe-stem through it. An even more grotesque and, to us, revolting ornament was the labret worn by the Tlingit and Haida women of the northern half of the coast. It was an oval plug of wood, bone, or even stone with a concave edge, worn in a hole made in the lower lip. Some labrets were quite small but the larger ones, sometimes more than an inch across, were heavy enough to weigh the lip down so that it turned outward and hung upon the chin.

The labret wearers left their heads as nature made them, however. The Nootka flattened their foreheads by binding a padded board to them in infancy, and the Kwakiutl bound babies' heads all the way around. This changed the shape of the brain without apparently injuring it and the pointed head was considered a vast improvement upon nature.

Haida woman wearing a nose ring and a labret

Shamans

It's difficult to think of the beliefs of the North-west coast Indians as a religion; it was merely a multitude of fears and hexes. They acknowledged some vague gods but they gave them scant attention. Since they believed in the immortality of animals, they assumed survival after death for man also, but their conceptions of the next world

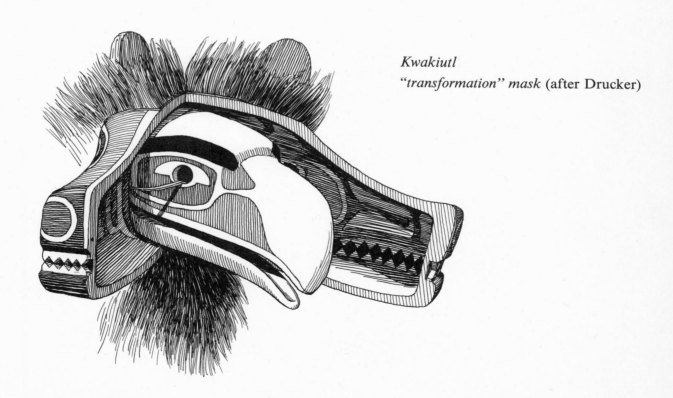

Kwakiutl "transformation" mask (after Drucker)

Shaman "resurrecting" a "dead" man

would never persuade anyone, whatever his lot, to wish to shorten his stay in this one.

In addition to the legendary animals who were "ancestors" and the semi-deified food animals, who were considered deliberately beneficent to man, there was a weird calendar of malicious spirits in animal form, or something near it. It was the shaman's duty to encourage the good spirits and to pacify or subdue the evil ones. Thus he could assure the seasonal return of the salmon and the otter. He performed his chores with great gusto, and because there was plenty of leisure to prepare such things, he put on elaborate and fearsome performances.

You might have found it hard to love a shaman. He was deliberately unkempt and glowered upon the world from under a matted tangle of hair. He was physician, priest, and necromancer and there was no sharp distinction between his functions. He was really good at sleight of hand and he used

as much mechanical equipment in his performances as any modern magician or medium. The shows were staged indoors with the help of the members of a secret society. Costumed actors wearing exaggerated masks represented the demons. The masks were beautifully carved; many of them had movable parts controlled by strings. Some were even masks-within-masks by means of which transformations could be staged. Seen in the flickering firelight of a smoky room, they might disturb an observer more sophisticated than an Indian schooled to believe in their reality.

The shows were more than masked pageants; all sorts of supernatural things took place. Small wooden images that couldn't be identified as such sailed through the air. By means of kelp speaking tubes, ghostly voices were heard high in the rafters of the house. Stooges became possessed of demons that were duly exorcised after the possessed one had made a point of biting someone. Men were

150

"killed" with great effusions of "blood" and were restored to complete health by the appropriate gestures of the shaman.

Along with all this, there were dances to a measure accented by rattles and by thumping on boxes and on long, hollowed-out planks that served as drums. People in the audience were sometimes carried away by it all and mounted to the house roof to drum enthusiastically on its planks. If their efforts split a plank, they gave the house chief a small token that would later be redeemed with a new plank.

Wealth and Prestige

Though these were warlike Indians, they could not attain honors by conspicuous valor as the Plains tribes did. A man's social standing was attained by birth and upheld by wealth. Sometimes it could be advanced by acquiring property. These things were true of no other Indians. The four social grades were: slave, commoner, noble, and chief (or king, as some old writers put it). A man's standing was recognized not only by his own town and clan but by other groups as well.

The way to demonstrate the possession of wealth was to give it away. When a man inherited a chieftainship he established his right to the position by holding a potlatch. The word is from the Chinook trade jargon that was used from the Columbia River to Alaska.

Basically, a potlatch was a feast, and by their attendance, the guests recognized the right of the host to his new honors. Potlatches could be given for other reasons: to assert formal claim to fishing rights, to celebrate a marriage, or even to reestablish the dignity of a notable who had suffered some humiliating accident. Each guest brought his own prestige with him and the seating of the visiting chiefs and nobles was regulated by protocol as rigid as that governing a State dinner.

A potlatch was a fine chance to make speeches and many community matters were settled. Children's ears were pierced and names were given to them; it was a good opportunity to announce names publicly. The right to use the crests of his wife's family would be claimed by and confirmed to a bridegroom who had paid the purchase price and was in good standing. Negotiations for other

marriages were conducted and considerable trading was done on the side lines.

Each guest of rank received gifts from the host. If any guest felt that he hadn't been treated with the respect due his importance, he made a gift *to* the host, who was expected to top it. The host might temporarily impoverish himself, but his turn as guest would come and he would be repaid at the potlatches of others. A host chief strove, by his munificence and by deliberately destroying property, to give the impression that a few possessions meant nothing to him. He would kill a slave or two and break up a couple of coppers to prove he could afford to do it.

A copper was one of the articles that represented wealth; it had no other use whatever. The metal was obtained from the Indians of the interior and was beaten into its characteristic shape, which seems to resemble nothing else and for which no explanation has been found. A copper was about three sixteenths of an inch thick and it might be three feet long, though that was exceptionally large. The object was given a considerable bulge parallel to its long axis. The lower half was rectangular; the upper half was the shape

Potlatch copper

of the high combs worn by Spanish ladies. A pronounced ridge separated the two halves, and a similar one divided the lower section vertically into two parts. Except for these ridges, the surface was decorated either by engraving or by painting; and sometimes there was a little embossing. Notable old coppers were given names and their value, enhanced by long trading, might reach the equivalent of several thousand dollars.

Fine skins, canoes, hand-woven blankets, and strings of rare shells were other evidences of wealth. The shells were dentalium, each about three inches long and shaped like an elephant's tusk. They were rare because they came from deep water and were hard to get. In the latter part of the 19th century the Hudson's Bay trade blanket became the principal potlatch item. Their chief's performance at the potlatch was a matter of vital importance to his townsmen, for his prestige reflected theirs. They frequently lent him

Guests arriving for a potlatch at a Haida village

goods to be given away and kept strict account of the loans and of the interest on them.

The large wooden food troughs mentioned earlier were made for potlatches. At the feast a family group would gather around each one, dipping in at will with big clam shells or carved dippers. What they couldn't finish on the spot, they took home with them. The stew was fish, perhaps dried salmon or fresh, depending on the season. On the side there would be salmon or herring roe in an advanced state of decomposition. Seal, porpoise, and whale meat would depend on season; so would a great delicacy: strawberries or raspberries beaten up with fish oil.

The great lack in the diet of these Indians was starch. Some camass root could be obtained in the south, but the northerners had to make out as well as they could with fat as a substitute. When Yankee sailing ships came to trade for sea-otter pelts, they found that their hardtack and molasses had high purchasing power.

These same ships brought diseases that killed off hundreds of Indians, so many that the social structure was disrupted. Chiefs died and left no heirs. Towns were depopulated to the point where it became wise to amalgamate with the remnants of other towns. It was then that the potlatches got out of hand and became fierce competitions between rival chiefs or between wealthy commoners striving to make chiefs of themselves.

Index

ABOUT THE AUTHOR

EDWIN TUNIS, well-known artist, illustrator, and muralist, was born at Cold Spring Harbor, New York. At present he is living near Shawan, Maryland, writing and painting. His most ambitious art project was a mural depicting the History of Spices, which took two years to paint and is 145 feet long. His articles have appeared in various magazines, and he has exhibited at the Baltimore Museum of Art, Society of American Etchers, National Academy of Design, Victoria and Albert Museum, and other well-known galleries. *Oars, Sails and Steam: A Picture Book of Ships,* his first book, was followed by his pictorial histories of *Weapons* and *Wheels.* His most recent book, *Colonial Living,* was awarded the Thomas Alva Edison Foundation Children's Book Award in 1958 for special excellence in portraying America's past.

THIS BOOK WAS SET ON THE FOTOSETTER IN

BASKERVILLE, TIMES ROMAN AND ALBERTUS TYPES BY

WESTCOTT & THOMSON

IT WAS PRINTED BY

COPIFYER LITHOGRAPH CORPORATION ON

PERKINS AND SQUIER COMPANY'S RR WOVE

MADE BY P. H. GLATFELTER COMPANY

THE BINDING WAS DONE AT

THE PRESS OF THE WORLD PUBLISHING COMPANY

TYPOGRAPHY AND DESIGN ARE BY

ERNST REICHL ASSOCIATES